THE AUGUSTAN REPRINT SOCIETY

GEORGE BICKHAM

THE
BEAUTIES *of* STOW

(1750)

Introduction by

GEORGE B. CLARKE

PUBLICATION NUMBERS *185-186*

WILLIAM ANDREWS CLARK MEMORIAL LIBRARY

UNIVERSITY OF CALIFORNIA, LOS ANGELES

1977

GENERAL EDITORS
William E. Conway, William Andrews Clark Memorial Library
George Robert Guffey, University of California, Los Angeles
Maximillian E. Novak, University of California, Los Angeles
David Stuart Rodes, University of California, Los Angeles

ADVISORY EDITORS
James L. Clifford, Columbia University
Ralph Cohen, University of Virginia
Vinton A. Dearing, University of California, Los Angeles
Arthur Friedman, University of Chicago
Louis A. Landa, Princeton University
Earl Miner, Princeton University
Samuel H. Monk, University of Minnesota
Everett T. Moore, University of California, Los Angeles
Lawrence Clark Powell, William Andrews Clark Memorial Library
James Sutherland, University College, London
H. T. Swedenberg, Jr., University of California, Los Angeles
Robert Vosper, William Andrews Clark Memorial Library

CORRESPONDING SECRETARY
Beverly J. Onley, William Andrews Clark Memorial Library

EDITORIAL ASSISTANT
Frances M. Reed, University of California, Los Angeles

INTRODUCTION

George Bickham, who published *The Beauties of Stow*, came from a family which has perplexed bibliographers. In the middle decades of the eighteenth century the Bickhams were well established as booksellers and publishers in London, but no more than a sketchy outline can be given of their history and not one of them can be identified with absolute confidence. Both the leading members of the family were called George, but several other Bickhams, with various names and initials, were connected with them, and it is not clear how many of these were real people and how many were aliases assumed in the devious course of their business. The two Georges may have been uncle and nephew, though it is perhaps more likely that they were father and son. George Bickham the Elder (?1684-?1758) was by profession a writing-master, though not one of the greatest, in an age when England's penmen led those of Europe; he was also an engraver—a very fine one of calligraphy—and a publisher. George Bickham the Younger (?1706-1771) seems not to have been trained to his father's profession but was described as having been at one time "drawing-master to the Academy at Greenwich"; he too became a publisher and an engraver, making his name with the topographical prints in which he specialized. For at least part of his publishing career he was associated with his father, but he habitually called himself "George Bickham Junior," and this must have been to establish his own professional identity. As publishers the Bickhams were enterprising, versatile, and none too scrupulous. The advertisement for the "Prints, and Books, Sold in *May's* Buildings," which filled out the last pages of *The Beauties* and is included at the end of this reprint, indicates the variety of their list: it ranged from topical pamphlets to manuals on geometry and dancing, from a picture book of famous horses to pocket diaries and educational toys—in short, they were prepared to publish anything that had a chance of finding a ready market. Nor did they hesitate to use other people's work when it suited them, a practice which provoked a number of successful actions against them in the Court of Chancery. In all this there is nothing to suggest that the Bickhams were any other than typical London publishers of Pope's generation.[1]

One of their books, however, has made them deservedly famous. This was *The Universal Penman*, which was announced for publication in 1733. In the previous half century hardly a year had passed without an important copy-book being published by individual writing-masters, but the Bickhams conceived the grand idea of printing a collection of all the finest contemporary hands in a single work, and they persuaded twenty-five writing-masters, including most leading ones of the day, to contribute. Furthermore, they thought up the ingenious scheme, familiar in the nineteenth century but unknown in their time, of publishing in periodical parts a work which they intended to issue subsequently in bound form. In practice, of course, their scheme proved hopelessly ambitious. Instead of taking fifty-two weeks to complete the project, it took eight years. Even so, *The Universal Penman* was a unique work, and its production made publishing history. So too did *The Beauties of Stow*, which appeared in 1750, but in a very different way.

Bickham's was not the first Stowe guidebook. Ever since about 1720, when Viscount Cobham had commissioned Sir John Vanbrugh and Charles Bridgeman, as architect and garden designer, to turn his father's house into a princely mansion with a more than princely garden, Stowe had attracted attention as one of the finest country seats in England. For thirty years Cobham continued to pour his fortune into it, particularly into the embellishment of the garden, employing one leading architect and designer after another, adding lakes and vistas and temples and statues, until the lay-out extended over more than a hundred acres and had become a showplace of Europe. But it was not just the sheer size of the garden and the multitude of its temples which attracted people. Cobham had made it a leading example of the new style of "natural" gardening initiated by William Kent, and in the generation when the gardening mania swept England every enthusiast wanted to see the improvements at Stowe. After 1733, when Cobham quarrelled with Walpole and George II and was dismissed from public office, the sophisticated visitor found a further attraction. For the ideals of the "Patriot" opposition spilled over into Cobham's gardening, so that his construction programme took on the character of a political manifesto. Thus the relish of satire was added to the satisfaction of aesthetic pleasure, and visitors walked round, notebook in hand, taking down the details of buildings and statues, and copying out the inscriptions for their journals.[2]

If ever a situation called for a guidebook, this was it, but none existed. Gilbert West, one of Cobham's nephews, wrote a topographical poem in praise of his uncle's garden published in 1732,[3] and a couple of years later Bridgeman commissioned a series of superb engravings to illustrate the garden he had laid out.[4] These were both desirable books for a gentleman's library, but they were not designed for the tourist and were of no use during a perambulation of the garden. Indeed, though several accounts of journeys through Britain appeared in print during the 1720s, and though the most famous of these travellers' guides, Defoe's *Tour Thro' the Whole Island*, ran to several editions, guidebooks to single places, which existed in Italy and which we now take for granted, were a genre very nearly unknown in England at that time.[5] The closest equivalents were two publications issued for Wilton and Houghton: Gambarini's *Description of the Earl of Pembroke's Pictures* (1731) and Horace Walpole's *Aedes Walpolianae, or a Description of the Collection of Pictures at Houghton Hall in Norfolk* (1743). But though Walpole included two plans and elevations and briefly described many of the rooms, both these books, as their names imply, were essentially catalogues of the pictures for connoisseurs. In spite of the increasing popularity of country house visiting during the first half of the eighteen century, publishers were slow to see the potentialities of the tourist trade, and it was left to another enterprising writing-master, Benton Seeley of Buckingham (the small country town three miles from Stowe), to produce the first comprehensive guidebook to an individual country seat.[6]

Seeley's model, or at any rate his inspiration, must have been the account of Stowe which appeared in the appendix to the 1742 reprint of Defoe's *Tour*. Most of this appendix was taken up by the accounts of six gardens, which were there described in detail for the first time, with a note that they were to be "incorporated in their proper places, in future editions of this work"—an innovation which reflected a new demand from the touring public. No fewer than sixteen of the thirty-two pages were devoted to Stowe, and these were adapted by Seeley and re-arranged into a sequence which followed the normal circuit of the gardens. So, in 1744, *A Description of the Gardens of Lord Viscount Cobham at Stow* was published as an octavo pamphlet of thirty-two pages, printed by W. Dicey of Northampton and sold by "B. Seeley, Writing-Master, in Buckingham, and George Norris, Peruke-Maker, in Newport-Pagnell, Bucks."[7] Intentionally it was an objective catalogue, all comment, such as existed in Defoe's *Tour*, being carefully excluded. In a short preface Seeley claimed that he was providing "a plain Account...a simple, regular Relation of every Thing in Order." Such a description, he went on, had often been enquired for, and he presented it to the public "with this View only, that it will save the Trouble of taking down the Inscriptions, or the Names of the Buildings, and be an Help to the Memories of those Numbers who have the Curiosity to see these Gardens."

This modest venture met, in Seeley's own words, with "great, and indeed unexpected, Success," which presumably included the approbation of Stowe's noble owner, for in the following year (1745) an expanded edition of thirty-four pages appeared, with a fulsome dedication to Lord Cobham in place of the original preface. Further editions were needed in each of the years up to 1749, all of them "corrected and enlarg'd" to keep pace with the continuous expansion of the gardens, though by resetting the type the thirty-four pages were again reduced to a more convenient thirty-two. Things had clearly gone well for Seeley, who changed the description of himself on the title page from "writing-master" to "bookseller and stationer," dropping George Norris from the partnership and making arrangements for his guidebook to be available in London, at Rivington's in St. Paul's Churchyard. Encouraged by his success, he embarked on a fresh venture. In 1747 he had published a sermon preached at Buckingham by William Gilpin, and in the following year he brought out *A Dialogue upon the Gardens at Stow*, an octavo pamphlet of sixty-four pages by the same author, following it with a second, revised edition in 1749. This remarkable work by the youthful Gilpin, which has already appeared under the imprint of the A.R.S., contains what may be the earliest criticism of landscape in terms of the picturesque and is an important document of aesthetic theory.[8] But Seeley's intention in publishing it was more practical. What he wanted was a companion piece to his factual *Description*, and this was what was provided by the running commentary of the two gentlemen who made the circuit of the gardens in the *Dialogue*. A year later the range of Seeley's Stowe publications was extended still further by a set of *Views of the Temples and other Ornamental Buildings in the Gardens*. These engravings varied in size, many being quite small and appearing six together on the octavo page; though crude, they were accurate enough to identify the buildings and to remind visitors afterwards of what they had seen. Several of the plates were dated May 1st 1750, and the set, with its engraved title page, must have been on sale soon afterwards, for Sanderson Miller noted in his account book that he had purchased "Seely's Prints of Stowe" on July 10th of that year.[9]

In the summer of 1750, therefore, three of Seeley's publications on Stowe were available in Buckingham and London: the *Description* for sixpence, the *Dialogue* for a shilling, and the *Views* for two shillings and sixpence. Bound up together with a combined title page, they cost five shillings. By providing for the increasing flood of tourists Seeley had created a profitable sideline for himself, but the monopoly he had hitherto enjoyed was about to come to an end. Later in the same year George Bickham brought out *The Beauties of Stow*, the volume here reprinted. The exact date of its publication is not known, but it was noted in the monthly catalogue of books in *The London Magazine* for October 1750. Nor is it certain which George Bickham was concerned, though it is likely that the younger one, who did the engravings, was responsible for the whole production. The octavo volume of sixty-four pages (including the advertisements) was printed and sold in London; and, like the bound version of Seeley's pamphlets, it was priced at five shillings.

Bickham's aim was to combine in a single volume the whole range of material that Seeley was offering in three, and to present it in a more attractive and personal way, as if someone who knew the gardens well were accompanying the visitor on his rounds, guiding him from one feature to another and pointing out the interest and merits of each in turn. All the temples were clearly named and described, with the inscriptions and their translations printed in full;[10] nearby was an illustration, usually full page, of the building concerned. Instead of hunting through Seeley's three pamphlets for the relevant information, the visitor with *The Beauties* found everything together in one place, and a brief description of the house was thrown in as well. There was little Seeley could do about it, and in the following year he tacitly admitted Bickham's superiority by converting the third edition of Gilpin's *Dialogue* into a narrative with the inscriptions included as footnotes; at the same time he re-issued his *Views*, engraving on the old plates the page numbers referring to this new edition. But it was a lame imitation of *The Beauties*. Seeley had been outmanoeuvred and retired temporarily from the contest.

Bickham's ascendancy was confirmed in 1753, when he published a set of his own topographical engravings of Stowe, a project well outside the range of a country bookseller like Seeley. These views were based on original drawings commissioned from J-B. Chatelain and engraved by himself. He dedicated them to Earl Temple, thereby no doubt ingratiating himself with the new owner of Stowe, and in the same year he brought out a revised edition of The Beauties. The text remained unaltered, but two of the illustrations were brought up-to-date; and, what was more important, there was included for the first time a "Curious General Plan of the Whole Gardens." Bickham had also made arrangements for the guidebook to be available locally. Printed and sold in London, it could also be bought from "Mr. Hoskins at the New Inn going into ye Gardens. Where may be had the 16 Perspective Views Price 1 Guinea Plain & 2 Guineas Coloured."

But it was not just Bickham's professional expertise as a publisher and engraver that enabled him to cut Seeley out of the Stowe tourist market and supplant him in its owner's favour. There is more than a suspicion that he was guilty of sharp practice too. After Cobham's death in September 1749 there was an interregnum of over a year before his nephew and successor, Richard Grenville (soon to become Earl Temple), was firmly established in control of affairs at Stowe. During this period, when Seeley had lost his old patron's protection, the way was open for opportunists to break in, and at least two plagiarized editions of his guidebook are known to have been published at about this time in Oxford, probably at the instance of a local innkeeper. Though these would have caused Seeley no more than temporary embarrassment, the case was different when it involved a well-known London publisher like Bickham. There was no preface to The Beauties, but in a passage (p. 63) containing the sort of remarks generally found there Bickham openly admitted that he had "made use of some Descriptions already printed." If he had been accused of drawing too freely on other people's accounts, he would probably have argued, as others had before him, that accuracy, not originality, was what was required in a guidebook.[11] But when The Beauties is examined in detail, it becomes clear that he was using previously published works on a scale that was tantamount to piracy.

Analysis indicates that the author of The Beauties had in front of him four different accounts of Stowe, all printed in 1748: the fifth edition of Seeley's Description, the first edition of Gilpin's

Dialogue, the fourth edition of Defoe's *Tour Thro' the Whole Island*, and *Les Charmes de Stow*, a French description published in London, but of uncertain origin.[12] Whereas *Les Charmes* provided the title and subtitle of *The Beauties*, the plan of the book was taken from the *Description*, the author following Seeley's circuit exactly, as on the redrawn map of the gardens (*See Map and Key following*). Sometimes he transcribed extended passages from one or another of his sources, at other times he dovetailed together short sections from several, an operation requiring numerous minor alterations to the text.[13] He also had to add some brief linking passages ("Near this bridge is...," "Now, as you walk along, you come to...," etc.), though many of these too he was able to take over unchanged, usually from the *Tour*. Even the editorial remarks on page 63, explaining "the Reason why I thought this work would be acceptable to the Public," prove on examination to be adapted from a passage in *Les Charmes*. Within his self-imposed limits the author worked with considerable success, conveying the information accurately and giving his guidebook a convincing personal tone. This is particularly true of the first twenty pages or so. Later on, perhaps because he grew weary or was in a hurry, he became careless, confusing his pronouns, repeating the same facts about a building further down a page, and not pausing long enough to reconcile two slightly contradictory accounts. It would be tedious to detail all his borrowings. The matter can be summed up by stating that the overwhelming majority of the 1784 lines in *The Beauties* were lifted from one or another of the four texts already mentioned: 589 lines (33% of the whole) from the *Description*, 647 lines (36%) from the *Dialogue*, 324 lines (18%) from *Les Charmes*, and 187 lines (11%) from the *Tour*. There are fewer than 40 lines (2%) for which no printed source has been traced, and only these require further investigation.

Two such passages—the opening lines on the approach road to Stowe (p. 1) and the reference to the Monument in London (p. 59)—do not imply any local knowledge and can be set aside. There are, however, several things which could hardly have been discovered except on a visit to the gardens. From other evidence it is known that the former vicar was "Con. Rand" (p. 25) and that the ridings were "Eight or Ten Miles round" (p. 60), but these facts are recorded here in print for the first time. And this is the only source of the convincing suggestions that the paintings in the Witch-House were "copied from the famous *Gillot's*

Prints" (p. 24) and that the reliefs in the Temple of Contemplation represented "*Caesars* Heads" (p. 32). On the same page (ll.3-11) there is a longer passage describing in detail the rococo features in front of the Grotto, and this useful information too is almost certainly correct. On the other hand, three other statements — that the Cascade "will run at any time Nine Hours" (p. 4), that the Alto-Relievo on the backside of the Palladian Bridge was by Rysbrack (p. 50), and that the house was "Ninety odd Yards long" (p.64) — are just as certainly wrong. And the seven lines on the Grecian Temple (pp. 47-48), a building about which it would be valuable to have first-hand information in 1749-50, are obviously garbled. Where does this odd mixture of truth and error come from? The most likely source is perhaps the fly-leaf and margins of a guidebook, where a visitor jotted down what he himself had observed and what he had been told by some talkative estate gardener, that perennial fount of half-truth and gossip.

But, even if this conjecture is correct, the marginal notes cannot have been written by the author of *The Beauties*, for the evidence makes it clear that the author had never set foot in the gardens. Had he ever visited Stowe and seen the rusty ironstone of which the Gothic Temple is built, he would not have paraphrased Seeley's "red stone" as "brick." Had he himself seen the couches inside the Sleeping Parlour, he would not have made the blunder of translating as "canopies" the word "canapés" which he found in *Les Charmes*. And if he had ever seen the Chinese House with his own eyes, he would not have described it as square "according to the Drawing, or Print," nor made an equally ingenuous remark about the Egyptian Pyramid. Still less, if he had walked the circuit of the gardens himself, would he have led the visitor to the Grenville Column at the northern end of the lay-out and then jumped straight to the Palladian Bridge at the southeast corner (p. 50). "Not far from this, and up a grand Walk," he remarked confidently, "I am leading you now to that genteel Piece of Building...." But in fact it is a full half-mile to the Palladian Bridge as the crow flies, no direct path then led there, and there is a steepish hill in between. What he had done was to follow Seeley blindly, mistakes and all. In Seeley's case the error was more pardonable, for since he had first established his route round the gardens in 1744 several new buildings had been put up on this eastern side, and by directing the visitor to look at them he had broken the line of his circuit. Seeley was aware of it and worked out a new route for his 1749 edition, but the author of The Beauties was not to know this, since he travelled no further than his study to compile the guidebook's text.

The case of the illustrations is somewhat different. There must be a direct connection between Bickham's engravings and those in Seeley's Views, for some of the illustrations are identical and others are mirror images, and it is hardly to be doubted, after analysing the text, that Bickham was copying Seeley and not vice-versa. This is established almost beyond question by several of the captions, which are the same as those under Seeley's engravings but do not tally with the descriptive titles in the text of The Beauties. It may be presumed, therefore, that Bickham had a copy of Seeley's Views in front of him on his drawing table as he worked. But it is not quite so simple as that. Almost all Bickham's engravings are larger than Seeley's and more detailed. There is no effective illustration of the garden landscape, nothing more than a background of conventional foliage to the buildings. But though some of the additional details could have been pure fantasy, and some made up to illustrate the description in the text, there are other engravings which seem convincingly more accurate than Seeley's; furthermore, two buildings, the Saxon Temple and the Castle, have no counterpart in Seeley's Views. The most reasonable explanation is that Bickham himself toured Stowe with Seeley's Views in his hand, making sketches and notes to amplify those that were inadequate as models for his own engravings.[14] Indeed, it is tempting to suggest that it was Bickham who jotted down comments in the margin of his own guidebook as he went round, and that afterwards he bought up all the other tourist publications he could find, paying some Grub Street writer to run them together into a single account.

What it amounts to is this. The text of The Beauties is a conflation of all the printed accounts of Stowe available in 1748. In general it is accurate but almost wholly derivative, and, except in the handful of passages already discussed, cannot be regarded as independent evidence on the buildings or gardens. The illustrations too are strongly influenced by those previously published, but somewhat more confidence can be placed in them, for there is reason to believe that Seeley's Views, before being copied or modified, had been compared on the spot with the actual buildings. An officious regard for truth, however, was not one of Bickham's characteristics. He used the Views, like Seeley's other publications, for his own purposes with cynical lack of scruple, and, as if to make his attitude absolutely obvious, when he came to engrave the plate of the Egyptian Pyramid (p. 9), he omitted Cobham's fine epitaph on Vanbrugh and replaced it with a comment of his own. Inscribed on the stonework is the line "SEELEY IS A ****." The four letters of the last word are half obliterated, but they can be supplied by readers according to taste.

As it turned out, Bickham had underestimated his provincial rival. After a short interval Seeley entered the field again. This time, having learned from experience, he was a more formidable opponent. Prudently he joined forces with his London bookseller, becoming the junior partner, and his next guidebook (1756), containing a map of the gardens which was a decided improvement on Bickham's, was printed in London for "J. Rivington in St Paul's Churchyard, and B. Seeley in Buckingham." In the same year, presumably to counter this threat, Bickham brought out a revised edition of *The Beauties*, correcting errors in the illustrations and text, and omitting several passages of doubtful relevance. Sold in London and at the New Inn, this "much improved" edition was certainly the best guidebook then available. But Bickham's position was undermined a year or two later, when the inn changed hands again and the new proprietor, Mr. Hodgkinson, joined Rivington and Seeley in a partnership which was to last for twenty years. Their 1759 guidebook introduced an entirely new feature, a tour of the principal rooms in the house with details of the pictures and the interior decoration. In reply, Bickham took over their material, re-arranged it in a different order and printed an eight-page supplement which was bound in, rather clumsily, with his existing guidebook. But he had lost the initiative, and when Seeley brought out two more editions in quick succession, in 1762 and 1763, corrected and brought up to date to take account of yet more alterations to the buildings and gardens, Bickham retired for good from the Stowe scene.[15] The battle of the guidebooks was over.

This is the appropriate place to bring the present account to an end. Seeley and his family were to continue publishing the Stowe guidebooks for the next seventy years. Before long, as their business expanded, they were to establish their own printing press in Buckingham and set up as publishers in London, where their firm is still flourishing two centuries later.[16] In other fields too they were to make their name, producing a number of authors and scholars in the nineteenth century, of whom Sir John

Seeley, the great historian, was the most distinguished. But 1763 marked the moment of Benton Seeley's triumph. Not only had he finally ousted his rival, but his guidebook of that year was a work of outstanding merit in its own right. All the expected things were there, including a well documented tour of the house and gardens, a clear plan of the gardens, and good illustrations of all the buildings, many of them specially redrawn. But there were also novel additions: an elevation of the garden front of the house, drawn to scale, together with a plan of all the important rooms on the principal floor, and measured drawings of no fewer than twenty-one of the garden buildings.[17] Every ingredient that an intelligent visitor could ask for was contained in this edition, which may be considered a model of what such a thing should be. How many of today's guidebooks contain as much?

Yet the astonishing fact is that by this date no comprehensive guidebook had been published for any other country seat in England. Many great houses and gardens were attracting tourists—Blenheim, Hagley, Holkham, Kew, the Leasowes, Stourhead, for example—and guidebooks were to be produced for all of these before the end of the century, but none had appeared by 1763.[18] The genre evolved and reached near-perfection at Stowe in virtual isolation, and most of the credit for this achievement can be claimed for Seeley. A little should go to Rivington, who helped him at a critical point in his struggle; more, perhaps, to the two enlightened owners of Stowe, the Lords Cobham and Temple, who gave him their patronage. But some share of the credit must be allowed, however grudgingly, to George Bickham. Had it not been for the challenge presented by this London interloper, with his expertise, his nose for the market and his sheer effrontery, it may be doubted whether Benton Seeley, the country writing-master, would have been inspired to go on improving his guidebook, edition after edition, until he had outdistanced any possible rival. *The Beauties of Stow* may be a disreputable little volume, but it remains a milestone in the development of tourist literature.

Stowe

NOTES TO THE INTRODUCTION

1. On the Bickham family see Ambrose Heal, *The English Writing Masters and Their Copy-Books, 1570-1800* (Cambridge: First Edition Club, 1931), pp. 14-17; P. H. Muir, "The Bickhams and their *Universal Penman*," in *The Library* (Transactions of the Bibliographical Society), XXV (1945), 162; Philip Hofer, foreword to the facsimile edition of *The Universal Penman* (Jericho, N.Y.: Paul A. Struck, 1941).

2. For a brief historical account of Stowe's house and gardens see the series of articles in *Apollo* (June, 1973).

3. *Stowe, the Gardens of the Right Honourable Richard Lord Viscount Cobham* (London, 1732), published anonymously but known to be by Gilbert West.

4. Fifteen views of Stowe drawn by Jacques Rigaud, *c.*1734, and engraved by himself and Bernard Baron; issued by Sarah Bridgeman, the designer's widow, in 1739, with a map of that date; published for binding up, with a title-page, by Thomas Bowles (London, 1746).

5. One isolated early example is known (*A Brief Description of the House and Garden of Josiah Diston, Esq. at Epsom in Surrey*, 1726); and in 1745 *A Plan of Mr. Pope's Garden* was published with accompanying notes by his gardener, John Searle.

6. See John Harris, "English Country House Guides, 1740-1840," in *Concerning Architecture: Essays on Architectural Writers and Writing presented to Nikolaus Pevsner*, edited by John Summerson (London: Penguin Press, 1968) pp. 58-74; republished in a revised form in *A Country House Index* (Shalfleet Manor, Isle of Wight: Pinhorns, 1971); to be revised and reprinted with additions, 1977. Though my conclusions are not always the same as Mr. Harris', my work on this subject is based on his, and I am greatly indebted to him for his help on a number of problems.

7. The reason for the Newport Pagnell connection is not known, but Benton Seeley (?1716-1795) may have been a native of that town. Mr. G. R. Elvey informs me that a bookseller and stationer who died there in 1784 was called Leonard Seeley.

8. See John Dixon Hunt's introduction to A.R.S. No. 176. Both the sermon and the *Dialogue* were published anonymously, but the case for Gilpin's authorship has been convincingly argued by William D. Templeman, *The Life and Work of William Gilpin* (Urbana: University of Illinois Press, 1939), pp. 33-35, 117-129.

9. Warwick County Record Office, CR 1382/1. Sanderson Miller was using a copy of *The New Pocket, or Memorandum-Book* published by George Bickham.

10. The only omission, presumably by an oversight, was the dedicatory inscription on the Temple of Ancient Virtue ("Priscae Virtuti").

11. See Esther Moir, *The Discovery of Britain: The English Tourists, 1540 to 1840* (London: Routledge & Kegan Paul, 1964), pp. 24-25.

12. The full title-page is as follows: "Les / CHARMES / de / STOW: / ou / DESCRIPTION / de / La belle Maison de Plaisance / de / Mylord COBHAM / par / J. d. C / à LONDRES, / Chès J. Nourse, 1748." It cost one shilling. The origin of this book is obscure. It was noted by its main title in the booklist of the *Gentleman's Magazine* for June 1749; in the same month the booklist of the *British Magazine* noted the title and subtitle, adding the phrase, "avec une traduction angloise, a Cote." No copy with an accompanying English translation has come to light, but several passages are so similar to Gilpin's *Dialogue* that there must be a connection between them.

13. The following pages of *The Beauties* contain extended borrowings of half a page or more, though lines from the other source books are frequently inserted there too:
    From the *Dialogue*: pp. 2-3, 5, 6, 22, 25-26, 32-35, 36, 38-39, 51, 54-56, 59-63.
    From the *Tour*: pp. 8-9, 37.
    From the *Description*: pp. 11-15, 17-18, 26-29, 40-46, 49-50, 58-59.
    From *Les Charmes*: pp. 29-30, 46-48, 57, 63, 64-65, 65-67.
    For a sample page containing brief extracts dovetailed together, see the Appendix at the end of these notes.

14. Bickham certainly used Rigaud's views (see Note 4) when he engraved the "Perspective Views" of 1753, and he very probably had them before him when he was working on the illustrations to *The Beauties*, though they would have been of no use for the buildings in the Elysian Fields and the eastern part of the gardens, which were not illustrated by Rigaud.

15. Stowe continued to be featured in Bickham's *A Tour to Blenheim, Ditchley and Stow*, which ran to several editions under various titles. The elder Bickham is said to have died in 1758, and the younger in 1771, his stock-in-trade having been sold by auction at Richmond in 1767. See Heal, *op. cit.*

16. Seeley, Service and Cooper, of Shaftesbury Avenue, London.

17. These additions may have been prompted by Earl Temple, anxious that Stowe should keep pace with Kew, Holkham, and Houghton. Plans of the first two of these had been published, and of the third republished, in the previous two years.

18. So far as is known, the only comparable guidebook which may have appeared by 1763 is *A Description of the Gardens and Buildings at Kew*, published before 1771 but undated—and the co-author of that guidebook was the ubiquitous George Bickham.

APPENDIX

Page 16 of *The Beauties* is made up almost entirely of short excerpts from other accounts, which are printed below as a sample of the author's method. Italics indicate the borrowed passages.

"...*et de plus simple. Cela marque un Goût exquis dans le Génie qui préside ici.*" (*Les Charmes*, pp. 17-18)

"*The Temple of Bacchus.*" (Heading on p. 9 of the *Description*)

"*Leaving this Place, we approach a Building of a very different Nature—the Temple of Bacchus, built of Brick...*" (*Tour*, II, 221)

"...*& l'on ne manque guéres de s'y asseoir quelques momens, soit pour y reprendre haleine, soit pour en admirer la Peinture qui est très curieuse. On voit sur les murs le Triomphe de l'Yvresse & de la Joie; & sur le Plat-fonds le Dieu Bacchus d'une grosseur énorme. Les petites Figures sont excellentes...*"
(*Les Charmes*, pp. 14-15)

"...*painted by Mr. Nollikins.*" (*Description*, p. 9)

"*La vue est charmante tout autour de ce bel Edifice...*" (*Les Charmes*, p. 15)

"*Here we have a fine distant Prospect toward Aylesbury and Wendover Hills...*" (*Tour*, p. 221)

"*I am admiring the fine View from hence: so great a Variety of beautiful Objects, and all so happily disposed, make a most delightful Picture. Don't you think this Building too is a very genteel one, and is extremely well situated? These Trees give it an agreeable, cool Air, and make it, I think, as elegant a Retreat for the Enjoyment of a Summer's Evening, as can well be imagined.*"
(*Dialogue*, p. 14)

"In the Garden we have in full View the Temple of Venus; and between the two *is an Obelisk erected to the Memory of a Clergyman, with this inscription: To the memory of Robin Coucher*" (*Tour*, p. 222)

The line unaccounted for ("In the Front of this Building, and a little way from it") was probably added by the author after looking at the engraving facing page 16. In Seeley's *Views* the Temple of Bacchus and Coucher's Obelisk appear in separate engravings. Their relationship could have been observed by Bickham on the spot, or he could have seen them in Rigaud's engraving, where they are illustrated together.

KEY

1 Stowe House.
2 King George I's Statue.
3 Leoni's Arches.
4 The Cross Walk.
5 The Abele Walk.
6 The Octagon Basin & Guglio.
7 The Lake Pavilions.
8 The Grecian Temple (later Temple of Concord).
9 Captain Grenville's Monument.
10 Lord Cobham's Pillar.
11 The Lady's Temple (later Queen's Temple).
12 The Parish Church.
13 The Temple of Ancient Virtue.
14 The Temple of Modern Virtue.
15 The Vicarage.
16 The Witch House.
17 Apollo & the Muses.
18 The Grotto & Shell Temples.
19 The Temple of Contemplation.
20 The Chinese House.
21 The Shell Bridge.
22 The Temple of British Worthies (with inscription behind to "Signor Fido").
23 The Stone Bridge.
24 The Gothic Temple, and Saxon Deities.
25 The Palladian Bridge.
26 The Imperial Closet.
27 The Temple of Friendship.
28 The Pebble Alcove.
29 Congreve's Monument.
30 The Temple of Sleep, or Sleeping Parlour.
31 The Rotondo.
32 The Queen's Theatre & Statue.
33 King George II's Statue.
34 Dido's Cave.
35 The Temple of Bacchus.
36 Nelson's Seat.
37 The Boycott Pavilions.
38 The Pyramid.
39 Gibbs' Building, or the Belvedere.
40 The Temple of Venus.
41 The Hermitage.
42 The Cascade.
43 St. Augustine's Cave.
44 Coucher's Obelisk.

BIBLIOGRAPHICAL NOTE

The facsimile of *The Beauties of Stow* (1750) is reproduced by kind permission of Mr. Simon Houfe and the trustees of the late Sir Albert Richardson from their copy in the possession of Mr. Clarke. The total type-page (p. 7) measures 124 x 70 mm.

THE
BEAUTIES of *STOW:*
OR, A
DESCRIPTION
OF THE
PLEASANT SEAT,
AND NOBLE
GARDENS,

Of the RIGHT HONOURABLE

Lord Viscount COBHAM.

With above Thirty DESIGNS, or DRAWINGS, engraved on Copper-Plates, of each particular Building.

By *GEORGE BICKHAM.*

LONDON:

Printed by E. OWEN, in *Hand-Court*, opposite *Great Turnstile*, *Holborn*, for GEORGE BICKHAM, at his House and Shop in *May's-Buildings*, *Covent-Garden*. M.DCC.L.

A
DESCRIPTION
OF THE
GARDENS
Of the RIGHT HONOURABLE
The Lord Viſcount COBHAM,
AT
Stow, in *Buckinghamſhire.*

FROM *Buckingham* Town you paſs through a little Village called *Chatmore*, and from thence to the *New-Inn* at the South Entrance of the Garden, called *Stow.* This is a Proſpect, that agreeably ſurpriſes you ; for, upon quitting an unpleaſant Road, you perceive all at once a

B   long

long Avenue ; at the End of which rises a
fine View of my Lord's House, though a little
confin'd by the inward Row of Arbail-Trees.
This charming Garden you enter by Steps
that lead to a superb Terras, which is carried
crofs-ways the whole Length of the Ground.

TWO GRAND PAVILIONS.

On each Side of the Steps, there is an elegant Pavilion, built in an excellent Taste, and
painted in Fresco ; on one of which are represented the Adventures of *Dorinda* and *Sylvio* ;
on the other, that of *Myrtillo* and *Amaryllis*,
taken from *Pastor Fido*.— The disconsolate
Nymph there, poor *Dorinda*, had long been
in Love with *Sylvio*, a wild Hunter, of barbarous Manners ; in whose Breast she had no
Reason to believe she had raised an answering
Passion. As she was roving in the Woods,
she accidentally met his Dog, and saw her
beloved Hunter himself at a Distance hollow-
ing, and running after it : She immediately
calls the Dog to her, and hides it amongst
the Ruines. *Sylvio* comes up to her, and in-
quires very eagerly after the Dog ; the poor
Nymph puts him off, and tries all her Art to
inspire him with Love, but to no purpose ;
the cold Youth was quite insensible, and his
Thoughts could admit no other Object but
his Dog. Almost despairing, she at length
hopes

Boycoat Building.

From Page 8. to Page 6

Two of these Pavilions at the Entrance

Two of these Pavilions act entrance of ye Park

hopes to bribe his Affections, and lets him know she has his Dog; which she will return, if he will promise to love her, and give her a Kifs. *Sylvio* is overjoyed at the Proposal, and promises to give her Ten thousand Kiffes. *Dorinda*, upon this, brings the Dog: But, alas! fee there the Succefs of all her Pains! The Youth, transported at the Sight of his Dog, throws his Arms round its Neck, and lavishes upon it thofe Kiffes and Endearments in the very Sight of the poor afflicted Lady, which she had been flattering herfelf would have fallen to her Share.—In the other Pavilion, on this other Wall, is painted, *Difdain and Love have taken different Sides :* The Youth is warm, and the Nymph is coy. Poor *Myrtillo* had long loved *Amaryllis* ; the Lady was engaged to another, and rejected his Paffion. Gladly would he only have fpoken his Grief; but the cruel Fair-one abfolutely forbad him her Prefence. At length a Scheme was laid by *Corifca*, the young Lover's Conhdant, which was to gain him Admiffion into his dear *Amaryllis*'s Company. The Lady is enticed into the Fields, with fome of *Corifca*'s Companions (who were let into the Plot), to play at Blind-man's Buff; where *Myrtillo* was to furprife her. See there he ftands, hefitating what Ufe to make of fo favourable an Opportunity, which Love has put into his Hands. Painted by *Nollikins*.

The

The OBELISK.

From thence you descend to a large Octagon Piece of Water, with an Obelisk in the Centre Seventy Feet high, design'd for a *Jet d'Eau*; and distributes its Silver Veins, by the Help of Leaden Pipes, to the remotest Parts of the Garden : At a good Distance we behold two beautiful Rivers, which join, and enter the Octagon in one Stream. Here is such a Scene of Magnificence and Nature display'd, the Fields abounding with Cattle, the Trees and Water so delightfully intermingled, and such charming Verdure, Symmetry, and Proportion every-where presenting to the Eye, that the Judgment is agreeably puzzled, which singularly to prefer, of so many collected Beauties.

Then, turning on the Left-hand, you come to an artificial Piece of Ruins, which is mostly hid by a Clump of Ever-greens : It is adorned with the Statues of *Faunus*, *Satyrs*, and River-Gods ; a beautiful Cascade of three Sheets of Water, which will run at any time Nine Hours, falls from the Octagon, through Arches, into a large Lake of ten Acres : Just by, is a cold Bath.

But the Ruin is a great Addition to the Beauty of the Lake ; there is something so vastly picturesque and pleasing to the Imagination in such Objects, that they are a great

Addition

Artificial Ruin of Rockwork

Burlham Oct. 9ᵗʰ Oct. 1750.

Page 4.

The Hermitage

Page 5

Addition to every Landschape; and yet, perhaps, it would be hard to assign a Reason,
why we are more taken with Prospects of this
ruinous Kind, than with Views of Plenty and
Prosperity in their greatest Perfection? But
such Regularity and Exactness excites no
manner of Pleasure in the Imagination, unless
they are made use of to contrast with something of an opposite Kind. The Fancy is
struck by Nature alone; and, if Art does
any thing more than improve her, we think
she grows impertinent; and wish she had left
off a little sooner. Thus, a regular Building,
perhaps, gives us very little Pleasure; and yet
we find Rocks, beautifully set off in *Clara-
obscura*, and garnished with flourishing Bushes,
Ivy, and dead Branches, may afford us a
great deal; and a ragged Ruin, with venerable
old Oaks and Pines nodding over it, may
perhaps please the Fancy yet more, than either
of the other two Objects.

The HERMITAGE.

From hence we proceed to the Hermitage,
which is agreeably situated in a rising Wood,
and by the Side of the Lake: This old Hermitage, built all of Stone, at the Entrance of
a delightful Wilderness, has an exceeding good
Effect. It is of the Romantic Kind: And

Beauties

Beauties of this Sort, where a probable Nature
is not exceeded, are generally pleasing.

The TEMPLE of VENUS.

But let us ascend the Terras, and move towards the Left, which brings you to the Temple of *Venus*; with this Inscription, *Veneri
Hortensi*. It is a square Building, design'd
by Mr. *Kent*; the Inside adorn'd with Painting, by Mr. *Slater*; taken from *Spencer*'s
Fairy Queen.— The Lady is the fair *Hellinore*,
who, having left a disagreeable Husband, and
wandering in the Woods, was met by the
polite Set of Gentry she is dancing with :
She likes their Manner of Life, and resolves
to enjoy it with them.   Her old Spouse,
Malbecco, is inconsolable for his Loss ; he
wanders many Days in Search of her ; and at
length finds her (you see him at a Distance
peeping from behind the Tree) revelling with
a beastly Herd of Satyrs.   When the Evening
comes on, he follows the Company to their
Retirement, takes a convenient Stand, and to
his great Torment sees every thing that
passes among them.   After they were all laid
asleep, he creeps gently to his Lady ; and you
see him, in the other Painting, offering to be
reconciled to her again, if she will return
back with him : But *Hellinore* threatens to
awake the Satyrs,   and get him severely
handled,

Temple, dedicated to Venus.

Buckham Sculp ye Oct 7.50

Belvidere

Bickham Acc.t to Act 1750.

handled, if he does not immediately leave her. Upon which the poor Cuckold is obliged to fly, and foon after runs diftracted.—See Book III. Canto 10.

On the Outfide, are the Bufto's of *Nero*, *Vefpafian*, *Cleopatra*, and *Fauftina*; and, on the Frize, is the following Motto, alluding to the Painting.

> *Nunc amet qui nondum amavit;*
> *Quique amavit, nunc amet.*　　**Catullus.**

Let him love now, who never lov'd before;
Let him who always lov'd, now love the more.

The beft Judges muft fay, a Mafter has been at Work here! I cannot fay I have met with any modern Paintings, this long time, that have pleafed me better; I fee nothing to be cavilled at, with regard either to the Defign, Colouring, or Drawing: 'Tis true, the Stories arc a little loofe, the luxurious Couches or Sopha's, and the Embellifhment round the Walls, give the Piece quite a *Cyprian* Air, and make it a very proper Retreat for its incontinent Inhabitant.

The BELVIDERE.

But let us move forward towards yon Cubico-pyramidical Building, called the *Belvidere*;
the

the whole Use of which is to contribute to the different Vista's that terminate there, through a Thousand charming Alleys. It looks like a substantial one : However, it terminates this Terras exceeding well. The Ascent up to it, too, has a good Effect ; and so has the Field on the Right, its Beauties : How it strikes you at first Sight ! It is designed, like a Glass of Bitters before Dinner, to quicken your Appetite for the elegant Entertainment that is to follow : For my Part, I find it a very great Relief to my Eye, to take it from those grand Objects, and cast it for a few Minutes upon such a rural Scene as this ; and that Haycock contrasts extremely well with that Temple : Such Opposites, in my Opinion, are highly pleasing. Just here, is a fine Statue of the *Roman* Boxers.

BOYCOAT BUILDINGS.

From hence you come to Two Pavilions, or *Boycoat Buildings*, near the Entrance into the Park : Here are several agreeable Prospects into the Country : We see, on our Right-hand, a noble Terras: One of the Buildings is made use of as a Dwelling-house ; the other stands in a square Bottom, in the Garden ; and in the Inside of it are four Statues at full Length in Niches, *viz. Cicero, Faustina, Marcus Aurelius,* and *Livia.* The Buildings

are

Page 44

Egyptian Pyramid

SEE EYES AT EBIOS

are both finifhed with pyramidical Tops, by *Gibbs*. Betwixt them is a handfome Gateway, which is the Second Entrance to the Houfe ; from which leads up a noble Avenue, planted with double Lines of thriving Trees.

The *EGYPTIAN* PYRAMID.

From thence to the *Egyptian* Pyramid, which is Sixty Feet high, and about Half-way up, is this Infcription, in very large Chara&ers :

Inter plurima hortorum horum ædificia a Johanne Vanbrugh, *equite, defignata, hanc pyramidem illius memoriæ facram voluit* Cobham.

Among a very great Number of Stru&ures in thefe Gardens, defign'd by Sir *John Vanbrugh*, Knight; *Cobham* thought fit, that this Pyramid fhould be ere&ed to his Memory.

This Pyramid is made of Free-ftone, and all compofed of Steps, according to the Plate that grows narrow in proportion as they reach the Top. Underneath there is a low vaulted Chamber, which is quite empty, being fit for no other Ufe than as a Cave for the Dead. In it this Infcription :

Lufifti

Lusisti satis, edisti satis, atque bibisti.
Tempus abire tibi est ; ne potum largius æquo
Rideat et pulset lasciva decentius ætas.

HORACE.

With Pleasure surfeited, advanc'd in Age,
Quit Life's fantastic, visionary Stage :
Left Youth, more fitly frolicksome, may join
To push you, reeling, under Loads of Wine.

You cannot imagine how happily this Pyramid is situated, and what a beautiful Effect it has in different Points of Sight, and in the Deepening.

From hence, going along a Sort of Fortification-walk on your Left-hand, the Wood on the other hand, you enter the Field ; which is inclosed in a military Way, with a staked Fence : At the Angle, on the Middle of a Gravel-walk, are the Statues of *Hercules* and *Antæus.*

St. *AUGUSTINE*'s CAVE.

Hence we proceed to St. *Augustine*'s Cave ; which is a Building of Roots of Trees and Moss : Here you lose all the Sight of the Gardens, and of all its Beauties ; which are intercepted by Trees, Hedges, and a great Number of Shrubs. This is very artfully contrived ; in the same manner as Shades in a

Picture,

St Augustines Cave

Picture, or Pauses in Music. In this Cave
are a Straw Couch, a Wooden Chair, with
Three Inscriptions in *Monkish Latin* Verse.

On the Right hand :

Sanctus Pater Auguftinus
(Prout aliquis divinus
Narrat) contra fenfualem
Actum Veneris lethalem
(Audiat clericus) ex nive
Similem puellam vivæ
Arte mira conformabat,
Quacum bonus vir cubabat.
Quod fi fas eft in errorem
Tantum cadere doctorem ;
Quæri poteft, an carnalis
Mulier potius quam nivalis
Non fit apta ad domandum,
Subigendum, debellandum
Carnis tumidum furorem,
Et importunum ardorem :
Nam ignis igni pellitur,
Vetus ut verbum loquitur.
Sed innuptus hac in lite
Appellabo te, marite.

Saint *Auguftin,* holy Father,
(As from fome Divines we gather)
Againft the Sin of lewd Embrace,
And Act Venereal, his Grace

                              To

To fortify (Divines, give Ear,
The pious Precedent revere)
With wond'rous Art a Girl of Snow
Did make, the Life refembling fo,
That one from t'other fcarce you'd
    know.
This done, the good Man Side by Side
Lay down t'enjoy his new-form'd Bride.
But if a learned Doctor can
Fall, as might any other Man,
It may be afk'd, with Reafon good,
Whether a Girl of Flefh and Blood,
More certain far than one of Snow
Would not controul, fubdue, o'erthrow
The fwelling Rebel Flefh below;
Of Paffion cool the Rage and Boiling,
And hinder Nature from recoiling:
For Fire and Fire, two mortal Foes,
Expel themfelves, the Proverb goes.
But I unmarry'd, for Decree,
O marry'd Man, appeal to thee.

On the Left:

Apparuit mihi nuper in Somnio cum nudis et
anhelantibus molliter Papillis, & hianti fuaviter
Vultu——*Ehu! benedicite!*

Cur gaudes, Satana, *muliebrem fumere formam?*
Non facies Voti cafti me rumpere normam.
                               Heus!

Heus fugite in Cellam! pulchram vitate Puel-
*   lam ;*
Nam Radix Mortis fuit olim Fœmina in Hortis.

Vis fieri fortis? Noli concumbere Scortis.

In Sanctum Origenem Eunuchum.
Filius Ecclesiæ Origenes fortasse probetur ;
*   Esse Patrem nunquam se sine Teste probet.*

Virtus Diaboli est in Lumbis.

Satan, why, deck'd in Female Charms,
    Doft thou attack my Heart ?
My Vow is Proof againſt thy Arms,
    'Gainſt all thy Wiles and Art.
Ah! Hermits, flee into your Cells,
    Nor Beauty's Poiſon feed on.
——The Root of Death (as Story tells)
    Was Woman firſt in *Eden.*

Wouldſt thou thyſelf a dauntleſs Hero prove ?
Deteſt th' Enjoyments vile of lawleſs Love.

That *Origen*'s true SON of Church, agreed——
But could not for a FATHER be decreed.

In what we call the Loins, they ſay,
The Devil bears the greateſt Sway.

Fronting the Door :

Mente pie elata peragro dum dulcia prata,
*   Dormiit abſque dolo pulchra puella ſolo.*
C   *Multa*

Multa oftendebat, dum femifupina jacebat,
  Pulchrum Os, divinum pectus, aperta Sinum.
Ut vidi Mammas, concepi extempore Flammas,
  Et dicturus Ave, *dico,* Maria, cave :
Nam magno totus violenter turbine motus
  Pæne illam invado, pæne et in ora cado.
Illa fed haud lente furgit, curritque repente ;
  Currit, et, invito me, fugit illa cito.
Fugit caufa mali ; tamen effectus Satanali
  Internoq; meum cor vorat igne reum.
O Inferne Canis, cur quotidie eft tibi panis,
  Per vifus miros folicitare viros ?
Cur monachos velles fieri tam carne rebelles,
  Nec caftæ legi turbida membra regi ?
In tibi jam bellum dico, jam trifte flagellum,
  Efuriemque paro, queis fubigenda caro.
Quin abfcindatur, ne pars fincera trahatur,
  Radix, qui folus nafcitur ufq; Dolus.

As, loft in Thought, and Contemplation deep,
I wander o'er the verdant Meads——in Sleep ;
Sleep undefigning ; lo ! repos'd a Maid,
Frefh as the Verdure of her graffy Bed.
Reclin'd in Pofture half-fupine fhe lay :
A World of Beauties did her Form difplay :
Her Face, her Neck divine, her Bofom too,
With all their Charms, were open to my View.
Her heaving Globes no fooner ftruck my Eye,
But ftrait the Flames thro' all my Vitals fly.
I wou'd have faid my *Ave-Mary-Pray'r*,
But, 'ftead of that, I cry out, *Maid, beware.*

For,

For, in the Whirlwind of ſtrong Paſſion toſt,
And Reaſon in the vi'lent Tranſport loſt,
I almoſt ſeize the fair, inviting, Prey,
And to her Lips impatient urge my Way.
She ſudden ſtarts, and, with a rapid Flight,
Shoots from my Touch, and leaves my raviſh'd
　　Sight.
The Cauſe of Evil's fled—Th' Effect remains,
And furiouſly ſtill revels in my Veins:
Has kindled an infernal, fatal Flame,
Which inward burns thro' all my guilty Frame.
Why is't thy daily Food, O helliſh Cur!
Man up to Vice by wond'rous Sights to ſpur?
Why is't thy Pleaſure, *Monks* ſhould thus
　　rebel,
Their fleſhly Members 'gainſt their Laws
　　ſhould ſwell?
'Gainſt thee I now eternal War declare:
The Laſh ſevere, and Hunger, I prepare;
With theſe to mortify my carnal Luſt,
To theſe my Virtue, Chaſtity, to truſt.
But, left the Part, that's whole, ſhould be
　　infected,
That Modeſty may better be protected,
Beſt, once for all, to cut away the Root,
From which alone our guilty Paſſions ſhoot.

You ſee with what Art the Shades have
been managed throughout this magnificent
Picture; for, after having been raviſhed with
glittering and inchanting Objects, you ſud-
denly meet with others of a more ſoft and

C 2　　　　　　　　　　　ſimple

simple Kind : This implies an exquisite Taste in the presiding Genius of the Place.

The TEMPLE of *BACCHUS*.

Leaving this Place, you approach a Building of a quite different Nature, called, The Temple of *Bacchus*, built of Brick : Here one seldom misses sitting down a while, either to fetch a little Breath, or to admire the Painting. On the Walls you see the Triumphs of Drunkenness and Jollity ; and, on the Cieling, the God *Bacchus*, of an enormous Size. The small Figures are extremely well done, painted by Mr. *Nollikins*. Round this fine Structure, there is a delightful Prospect towards *Aylesbury* and *Wendover* Hills, with a great Variety of beautiful Objects ; and all, so happily disposed, make a most delightful Picture. These Trees give an agreeable cool Air, and make it, I think, as elegant a Retreat for the Enjoyment of a Summer's Evening, as can well be imagin'd. In the Front of this Building, and a little way from it, is an Obelisk erected with this Inscription :

To the Memory of ROBIN COUCHER.

The

Temple of Bacchus.

Coucher's Obelisk.

Bickham *sculp*t *to Oct* 1750

Nelson's Seat

Saxon Temple.

Bickham Sculp. I to Act?

The *SAXON* TEMPLE.

Not far from this is the *Saxon* Temple : It is an Altar placed in an open Grove, round which the Seven Deities of this Nation, that gave Name to the Days of the Week, were placed ; which are since removed to the *Gothic* Building, which we shall treat of in its Place.

*NELSON'*s SEAT.

The first Thing that strikes you here, is *Nelson*'s Seat. This is a small, but handsome oblong square Recess, in a Clump of Evergreens ; and is a well-painted Structure to the North-west of the Mansion-House, from whence there is an open Prospect ; and in it are the following Inscriptions, describing the Paintings, which are done masterly enough.

On the Right-hand :

Ultra Euphratem *et* Tigrim
usq; ad Oceanum propagatâ Ditione,
Orbis Terrarum Imperium Romæ *assignat optimus*
Princeps ;

cui fuperadvolat Victoria
Laurigerum fertum hinc inde
utraq; manu extendens,
comitantibus Pietate et Abundantiâ.

In Arcu Conftantini.

The moft excellent Prince,
having extended his Power beyond the *Eu-*
phrates and *Tygris*,
as far as the Ocean,
affigns the Empire of the World to *Rome* :
Over whom flies *Victory*,
ftretching forth a Laurel Crown
on each Side with both Hands,
accompanied with *Piety* and *Plenty*.

In the Arch of *Conftantine*.

On the Left :

Poft Obitum L. Veri
in Imperio cum Marco *confortis*,
Roma
integram Orbis Terrarum
Poteftatem ei, et in eo, contulit.

In Capitolio.

After the Death of *Lucius Verus*,
Partner in the Empire with *Marcus*,

Rome

Rome
conferr'd on him, and in him,
the whole Power over the World.
In the Capitol.

The Eye, after being confined in the Wood,
breaking at once out of it, we are agreeably
furprized with a fine open Country on the
North: On the South, the *Rotunda* appears:
On the Weft, the *Boycoat-Buildings* : On the
Eaft, the Equeftrian Statue (at the Head of the
Canal) of the late King ; which ftands in the
Front of the Houfe, with this Infcription :

In Medio mihi Cæfar *erit——*
Et viridi in Campo Signum de Marmore ponam
Propter Aquam. COBHAM.

Imperial *Cæfar* fhall the Centre grace ;
A Marble Statue to my Prince I'll place,
Near the clear Water, on the verdant Grafs.

Oppofite the South Front was the Parterre,
with the Statues of *Apollo* and the Nine Mufes,
which are now removed to the Spring of *Helicon*, for the Sake of the Profpect. The next
Object of View is a *Corinthian* Column, on
which is the Statue of his prefent Majefty,
with this Infcription :

G E O R G I O A U G U S T O.

Here

Here you have a moft delightful Profpect over the Country ; and, in the Garden, feveral of the Buildings prefent themfelves with great Pomp. The Lake, whofe Bounds are beautifully concealed, adds much to the general Agreeablenefs of the Place.

DIDO's CAVE.

Going from thence you find a dark winding Alley, which conducts you to *Dido*'s Cave. It is a retired dark Building of Stone in a Wood, and raifed on a Sort of Amphitheatre, with this Infcription :

Speluncam Dido, *Dux et* Trojanus, *eandem*
Deveniunt———————   VIRG.

Repairing to the fame dark Cave are feen
The *Trojan* Hero, and the *Tyrian* Queen.

Here you fee the pious *Æneas* at the Feet of his fair *Carthaginian*, both very lively reprefented ; and near them two handfome *Cupids* joining their lighted Torches, which are well drawn.

The

Didot Cave

Rotunda

The ROTUNDA.

Not far from hence a majeſtic Edifice riſes, called, The *Rotunda* : There is not a Piece of Stone-work in the whole Garden that makes a more beautiful Figure than this, in point of Perſpective; it is an airy Building, by Sir *John Vanbrugh*.   The Dome is ſupported on Ten *Ionic* Columns ; and, in the Centre, ſtanding on a circular Pedeſtal, is a *Venus à Medicis* : It ſtands on a gentle Riſe.

The late QUEEN's STATUE.

From this Place we have a View of Part of the Octagon, the Lake, the Fields, and ſeveral of the Buildings, preſenting themſelves alternately as we turn ourſelves round : On one Side you have an Opening, laid out with all the Embelliſhments of Art ; on the other, a ſpacious Theatre : Here you behold an Area, watered by a clear Canal, where wantonly ſport a vaſt Number of Swans and Wild-ducks. Her late Majeſty is the principal Figure in the Scene, with this Inſcription :

Honori, Laudi, Virtuti Divæ Carolinæ.

To the Honour, Praiſe, and Virtue of the Divine *Caroline*.

And

And around her a merry Company of Nymphs and Swains, enjoying themfelves in the Shade. This is abfolutely a moft charming Profpect, And then, on the oppofite Side, what a beautiful Contraft! for which we are almoft folely obliged to Nature. The Field is formed by that Semicircle of Trees into a very grand Theatre. The Point of Sight is centred in a beautiful manner by the Pyramid, which appears to great Advantage amongft thofe venerable Oaks; two or three other Buildings half hid amongft the Trees, which come in for a Share in the Profpect, and add much to the Beauty of it. Nor do I think this other View inferior to it: That Variety of Shades among the Trees; the Lake fpread fo elegantly amongft them, and glittering here and there through the Bufhes; with the Temple of *Venus*, as a Termination to the View. Here is a Vifto likewife, very happily terminated by the Canal, and the Obelifk rifing in the Midft of it. There is another clofe View likewife, towards *Nelfon's* Seat. In fhort, here is a Variety of very elegant Profpects, centred in this Point, which make up fome very beautiful Landfchapes. And, at fome Diftance thence, the Temple of *Sleep* unlocks its Gates, to draw you, as it were, from too great a Rapture of Admiration, and to afford you an Opportunity of recruiting your exhaufted Spirits, in order to be better able to examine, with Care, the

remaining

Sleeping Parlour

remaining Beauties of thefe inchanted Habitations.

The S L E E P I N G P A R L O U R.

This Temple is fituated at the Bottom of a lovely Recefs, contrived with all imaginable Art, in the Middle of a cool dark Grove; far from all Noife, and breathing, as it were, Tranquillity and Repofe. Six Walks centre in this Building, which is of Free-ftone; and contains only a middling Hall, where commodious Canopies invite you to fleep; and the Walls are adorned with moft charming Frefco's of the *Cafars* Heads, with feveral Feftons of Fruit, *&c.* On the Frife is this Infcription.

Cum omnia fint in incerto, fave tibi.

Since all Things are uncertain, indulge thyfelf.

I muft confefs, that I think *Ovid* himfelf could fcarce have buried the fenfelefs God in an happier Retirement. This gloomy Darknefs, thefe eafy Couches, and that excellent *Epicurean* Argument above the Door, would incline me wonderfully to indulge a little, if thefe beautiful Ornaments did not keep my Attention awake: But there wants a purling Stream, to fing a *Requiem* to the Senfes; though the Want is in fome meafure
made

made up by the drowsy Lullabies of that murmuring Swarm, which this Shade has invited to wanton beneath it ; and, I must own, Sleeping is a Compliment as much due to this Place, as Admiration and Attention are to *Raphael*, at *Hampton-Court*.

The WITCH-HOUSE.

Leaving this Place, and crossing the Avenue from the Pavilions before-mentioned, we come to the *Witch-House* ; which I look upon as a great Master-piece. You must know, that this House is inhabited by a Necromancer ; and that Inscription lets you know the Hand that has been employed to paint it. The Paintings are copied from the famous *Gillot's* Prints, called His Dreams. But here, the Composition, Drawing, and Pencilling, I must allow you, are not the most elegant ; but if the Design and Figures were the Artist's own (for they shew excellent Humour, and exceeding good Invention), that Consultation is well imagined; and so are these Witches and Wizards, their Employments likewise, their Form and Attitudes, are well varied : They are all painted by my Lord's Gentleman, and the Devices are alluding to the Name. This is a small Brick House, consecrated to Magic, Witchcraft, and Astrology. Care has been also taken to place in some Part of the Cave the famous
Tripod

Page 25

Tripod of the *Sibyl*. Not far from hence, is a House that formerly belonged to the Vicar *Con. Rand*, but now taken in the Gardens ; near the House, are placed on Pedeftals, *Apollo* and the *Nine Mufes*, round the Spring of *Helicon*. And now we proceed to the *Elyfian Fields* ; and here we have a View of a fine antique Building, call'd,

The TEMPLE of ANTIENT VIRTUE.

In this Rotunda, of the *Ionic* Order, done by Mr. *Kent*, you will find it a very illuftrious Affembly of great Men ; the wifeft Lawgiver, the beft Philofopher, the moft divine Poet, and the moft able Captain, that perhaps ever lived. I fancy you will hardly diffent from me, when I tell you thefe Heroes Names : There ftands *Lycurgus* ; there, *Socrates* ; there, *Homer* ; and there, *Epaminondas*. Illuftrious Chiefs, who made Virtue their only Purfuit, and the Welfare of Mankind their only Study ; in whofe Breafts, mean Self-Intereft had no Poffeffion. To eftablifh a well-regulated Conftitution, to dictate the foundeft Morality, to place Virtue in the moft amiable Light, and bravely to defend a People's Liberty ; were Ends, which neither the Difficulty in overcoming the Prejudices, and taming the favage Manners, of a barbarous State ; the Corruptions of a licentious Age, and the ill Ufage of an invidious City ; neither

D   the

the vaft Pains of fearching into Nature, and laying up a Stock of Knowledge fufficient to produce the noble Work of Art; nor popular Tumults at home, and the moft threatening Dangers abroad, could ever tempt them to lofe Sight of, or in the leaft abate that Ardency of Temper, with which they purfued them. This is an excellent Chace; for it would be difficult to trace, through all Antiquity, Perfons more eminent in the abovementioned Qualities, than thefe Four Heroes.

1. *EPAMINONDAS.*

Cujus a virtute, prudentia, verecundia,
Thebanorum refpublica
Libertatem fimul & imperium,
Difciplinam bellicam, civilem & domefticam
Accepit;
Eoque amiffo, perdidit.

Whofe Courage, Prudence, and Moderation, gave Liberty and Empire, an happy Eftablifhment, as well civil as military, to the *Theban* Commonwealth; but whofe Death fnatched from it the Enjoyment of thefe Bleffings.

2. *LY-*

2. *LYCURGUS.*

Qui summo cum consilio inventis legibus,
Omnemque contra corruptelam munitis optime,
Pater patriæ
Libertatem firmissimam,
Et mores sanctissimos,
Expulsa cum divitiis avaritia, luxuria, libidine,
In multa secula
Civibus suis instituit.

Having planned with the greatest Wisdom a political Constitution, secured by the most prudent means against every Inroad of Corruption, this great Father of his Country bequeathed to his Citizens the most lasting Liberty, and the severest Morals; the Gratification of every inordinate Desire being forbid by the Disuse of Wealth.

3. *SOCRATES.*

Qui corruptissima in civitate innocens,
Bonorum hortator, unici cultor DEI,
Ab inutili otio, & vanis disputationibus,
Ad officia vitæ, & societatis commoda
Philosophiam avocavit,
Hominum sapientissimus.

D 2　　　　　Whose

Whose Innocence of Life, and true Notions in Morality and Religion, withstood the Corruptions of a licentious State ; and whose Wisdom, and just Manner of thinking, delivered Philosophy from an idle and disputative scholastic Life, and introduced her into Society to amend Mankind.

4. HOMERUS.

Qui poetarum princeps, idem & maximus,
Virtutis præco, & immortalitatis largitor,
Divino carmine,
Ad pulchre audendum, & patiendum fortiter,
Omnibus notus gentibus, omnes incitat.

The first as well as best of Poets : Whose great and almost peculiar Excellence it was, that he made his Genius entirely subservient to the Cause of Virtue, and her Adherents ; instructing Mankind, by the Help of a Language universally known, in the godlike Arts of daring nobly, and suffering heroically.

Over one Door is this Inscription.

Charum esse civem, bene de republica mereri,
laudari, coli, diligi, gloriosum est : Metui vero,
& in odio esse, invidiosum, detestabile, imbecillum,
caducum.

To

To be dear to our Country, to deserve well of the State, to be honoured, reverenced, and loved, is truly glorious ; but, to be dreaded and hated of Mankind, is not only base and detestable, but highly impolitic like-wise, and hazardous.

And, over the other.

Justitiam cole & pietatem, quæ cum sit magna in parentibus & propinquis, tum in patria maxima est. Ea vita via est in cœlum, & in hunc cœtum eorum qui jam vixerunt.

Above all Things cultivate an honest Dis-position, and the benevolent, social Affec-tions ; which, confined within the small Cir-cle of our Friends and Relations, are indeed highly laudable ; but can then only be called truly virtuous and exalted, when they extend themselves wide enough to take in every In-dividual of the Society we are Members of. A Life so regulated, is the direct Road to the Regions of Happiness, and to the illustrious Assembly of those, who have thus benefited Mankind before us.

It is pleasing here to observe, that the Stone Steps which lead to the Temple Gate, as like-

wise

wife the Gate itfelf, are very narrow ; doubt-lefs, to infinuate the Difficulty of the Entrance. Another Thing very obfervable near this Tem-ple, is, a Heap of artificial Ruins ; which forms an admirable Contraft with this fine Building. The Explanation of the Enigma is this : This Temple reprefents the flourifh-ing State of Antient Virtue, which nothing has been able to impair or deftroy ; and which bravely defies the Power of Time. Thefe Ruins, and the old Statue juft clofe to them, are intended to fhew us the fhattered State of Modern Virtue ; which, as early almoft as its Birth, becomes withered and decrepit. Hence this fine Moral may be drawn, That Glory, founded on true Merit, is folid and lafting ; while a Reputation, built on the empty Ap-plaufes of the Multitude, foon fades away. This is really a juft and ingenious Thought. From this Spot we have no diftant Profpect ; but, notwithftanding that, it abounds with lafting Beauties : It is really placed in a Sort of Paradife ; and Things rifing adequate to that Name, you fee Friendfhip flourifhing in immortal Youth : Here are fweet purling Streams, refembling the melodious Sounds of Birds. We are now not far from the Parifh-Church, which is fo clofely furrounded with a Wood, as not to be feen. From hence you come to the Side of a River, where

Unpolifh'd

Temple of Modern Virtue.

Page 31

Grotto

Unpolilh'd Nature cannot boaft a Part:
For Chance too regular, too rude for Art.

And by its winding Banks, called, The Ser-
pentine River: At the Head of which is

The GROTTO.

The moft taking with every-body, and is the
moft charming Grotto that Imagination can
form.   Imagine you fee a fmall Edifice entirely built with Shells of Mother-of-Pearl ranged
with infinite Art, and with the Patience of
Penelope. The Infide confifts of one Hall, and
two Clofets, adorned in the moft furprifing
Manner ; and, at the fame time, in the moft
charming Tafte. The whole Place is full of
Mirrors fet in Mother-of-Pearl; by which the
Profpects of the Gardens, and of your own
Perfon, are infinitely multiplied. The Place
feems divided into a thoufand beautiful Apartments ; and appears Fifty times as large as it
is.   And the Sides of the Room are elegantly
adorned with Landfchapes, beyond the Pencil
of *Titian*; with this Advantage, that every View,
as you change your Situation, varies itfelf into
another Form, and prefents you with fome-
thing new. On each Side of this charming
Grotto there is a Temple, fupported one by
four wreathed, and the other by four ftrait
Pillars ; all compofed, as well as their Domes,

of

of Shells of Mother-of-Pearl of every Size
and Colour, and with Pebbles and Flints broken
to Pieces, which has a fine Effect. In the
Centre within is a Marble Statue of *Venus*, on
a Pedeftal. In the fame Tafte, in the Centre
of the two other Pavilions, are hugging *Cupids*
on Pedeftals. Before and between them is a
round tranfparent Pond, with gilded Carp, or
China Fifh ; which you command with your
Eye at any Part of the Bafon, and give a
great Addition to the Beauty of the Place,
fo juftly diftinguifhed by the Name of the
Elyfian Fields. From hence you proceed to
the Three-arched Building, called,

The TEMPLE of CONTEMPLATION.

Which.is a pleafant Recefs, by the Banks of
the River ;   and thofe Bas-Relievo *Cæfars*
Heads it is adorned with on the Infide, are
extremely good ones. And, I think, this *Ser-
pentine River*, as it is called, is a great Addition to the Beauty of the Place ; for Water
is of as much Ufe in Landfchape, as Blood is
in a Body ; without thefe two Effentials it is
impoffible there fhould be Life in either one
or the other : Yet, methinks, it is a prodigious Pity, that this ftagnated Pool fhould not
by fome Magic be metamorphos'd into a
cryftal Stream, rolling over a Bed of Pebbles.
Such a quick Circulation would give a Spirit
to the View. I could wifh they had fuch a
Stream

Temple of Contemplation

Published by Ino. Aikin Sept 1790

Stream at their Command ; they would fhew it, I dare fay, to the beft Advantage in its Paffage through the Gardens. But we cannot make Nature ; the utmoft we can do, is to mend her.

I have heard fpeak of the River, upon which the Town of *Stirling* ftands in *Scotland*, which as remarkable a *Meander* as I ever have heard of : From *Stirling* to a little Village upon the Banks of this River by Land it is only Four Miles ; and yet, if you fhould follow the Courfe of the Water, you will find it above Twenty. There is a Houfe likewife that ftands upon a narrow Ifthmus of a Peninfula, formed by this fame River, which is mighty remarkable : The Water runs clofe to both Ends of it, and yet will be carried a Compafs of Four Miles. Such a River, winding round about this Place, would make it Paradife indeed ! As we are got into the North, I muft confefs, I do not know any Part of the Kingdom that abounds with more elegant natural Views : Our well-cultivated Plains, as obferved before, are certainly not comparable to their rough Nature, in point of Profpect ; for fometimes you find yourfelf hemmed within an Amphitheatre of Mountains, which are varioufly ornamented, fome with fcattered Trees, fome with tufted Woods ; fome with grazing Cattle, and fome with fmoaking Cottages. Here and there an elegant View likewife was opened into the
Country ;

Country ; a Mile's Riding, perhaps, would
have carried you to the Foot of a fteep Pre-
cipice, down which thundered the whole
Weight of fome vaft River ; which was dafh-
ed into Foam at the Bottom, by the craggy
Points of feveral rifing Rocks : A deep Gloom
overfpreads the Profpect, occafioned by the
clofe Woods that hung round it on every
Side. I could fet down a Variety of other
Views to be met with there, if we here
wanted Entertainment in the way of Landfchape : One, however, I cannot forbear mentioning, and wifhing at the fame time, that
his Lordfhip had fuch Materials to work with,
and it could not be but he would make a moft
noble Picture. The Place, I am told, is upon
the Banks of the River *Eden* ; there is fcarce
known a fitter Place for a Genius in this way
to exert itfelf in. There is the greateft Variety of garnifhed Rocks, fhattered Precipices,
rifing Hills ornamented with the fineft Woods,
through which are opened the moft elegant
Vales that have ever been met with : Not to
mention the moft inchanting Views up and
down the River, which winds itfelf in fuch
a manner as to fhew its Banks to the beft Advantage ; which, together with very charming
Profpects into the green Country, terminated
by the blue Hills at a Diftance, make as fine
a Piece of Nature as perhaps can any-where
be met with. Now, all this is very romantic ;
but, at the fame time, I admire the Tafte in
Landfchape

Page 33 to 50.

Landfchape extremely ; and there are marked out juft fuch Circumftances, as would take me moft in View. Yet, though I can allow Nature to have an excellent Fancy, I do not think fhe has the beft Judgment ; though fhe is an admirable Colourift, her Compofitions are very often liable to Cenfure. For which Reafon I am for having her placed under the Direction of Art ; and the Rule I would go by, fhould be thus :

To treat the Goddefs like a modeft Fair ;
Not over-drefs, nor leave her wholly bare.

So let us leave thefe Flights, and view her here ; where fhe is treated according to the Prefcription of the Poet. And now, as we crofs that Alley, we are ftruck with the Sight of a pretty Building, called,

The *CHINESE* HOUSE.

It is fituated on Piles in the Middle of a River : You enter it by a Bridge, adorned with *Chinefe* Vafes, with Flowers in them : It is a fquare Building (according to the Drawing, or Print), with Four Lattices; and covered with Sailcloth to preferve the Paintings, which are done by Mr. *Sclater*. In my Opinion, it is a pretty Object enough, and varies our View in a very becoming Manner. Its cool Situation upon a River, and thofe Canvas-Windows
defigned

designed as well to keep out the Sun, as to let in the Air, give us a good Notion of the Manner of living in an hot Country : Within it is the Image of a *Chinese* Lady asleep; and all the Inside is *India* japann'd Work. Our Travellers tell us, the *Chinese* are very ingenious People, and that Arts and Sciences flourish among them in great Beauty : But, for my Part, whenever I see any of their Painting, I am apt, I must confess, in every thing else to call their Taste into Question : For it is impossible for one Art to be in Perfection, without introducing the rest : They are all Links of the same Chain : If you draw up one, you must expect the rest will follow. It is hardly to be imagined, that any Art, perfect in its Kind, would claim any Kindred, or even bear to keep Company, with such a wretched Art of Painting, as prevails amongst the *Chinese* : Its whole Mystery consists in daubing on glaring Colours. Correctness of Drawing, Beauty of Composition, and Harmony of Colouring, they seem not to have even the least Notion of. And we should certainly have some Productions of that Sort from *China*, if they were able to answer the Character I have sometimes heard given of them. They have very little of true manly Taste among them ; their Ingenuity lies chiefly in the Knick-knack Way. But hold ! We will walk again towards the River, and pursue it to the Canal : It is divided into Three

Parts :

Page 97

The Shudd Bridge

Parts : one takes its Rise from a dark-Wood,
another from the Grotto, and the Third to
the Pebble, or

SHELL-BRIDGE.

Which brings you into the *Elyſian Fields*, the
moſt charming Place that ever Eyes beheld.
It may not be improper here to give the following Lines, which were left by an unknown
Hand :

Charm'd with the Sight, my raviſh'd Breaſt
      'is fir'd
With Hints like thoſe, which antient Bards
      inſpir'd :
All the feign'd Tales, by Superſtition told,
All the bright Train of fabled Nymphs of old,
Th'enthuſiaſtic Muſe believes, are true ;
Thinks the Spot ſacred, and its Genius, you.
Loſt in wild Raptures, would ſhe fain diſcloſe
How, by degrees, the pleaſing Wonder roſe.
Induſtrious in a faithful Verſe to trace
The various Beauties of the lovely Place :
And, while ſhe keeps the glowing Work in
      View,
Thro' ev'ry Maze your artful Hand purſue——

The

The MONUMENTS of *BRITISH* WORTHIES.

Here you are prefented with an illuftrious Set of the greateft Wits, Patriots, and Heroes, that are to be met with in our Chronicles. This is an Edifice of a very fingular Tafte, without Roof or Gate, built in the Shape of a Quadrant : But when you view thofe Buftoes, or that awful Affembly, is not your Breaft warmed by a Variety of grand Ideas, which this Sight muft give Birth to ? There you have a View of the calm Philofopher, who fought Virtue in her Retirement, and benefited Mankind by Thought and Meditation. Some took the human Mind for their Theme ; examined the various Powers it is endowed with ; and gave us *to know ourfelves :* Others took Nature for their Subject, looked through all her Works, and inlarged our Notions of a God : While others, warmed with a generous Refentment againft Vice and Folly, made Morality their Care. To the cool Reafoner, ferious Philofcphy, without any Ornament but Truth, was recommended : To the gayer Difpcfiticn, the moral Song was directed, and the Heart was improved, while the Fancy was delighted : To thofe who were yet harder to work upon, the Force of Example was made ufe of : Folly is put to the Teft of Ridicule, and laughed

out

Temple of British Worthies. Bickham del.t to Oct. 1750.

out of Countenance ; while the moral Scene, like a diftorted Mirror fhews the Villain his Features in fo deformed a manner, that he ftarts at his own Image with Horror and Affright. On the other Side you are prefented with a View of thofe illuftrious Worthies, who fpent their Lives in Actions ; who left Retirement to the calm Philofopher, entered into the Buftle of Mankind, and purfued Virtue in the dazling Light in which fhe appears to Patriots and Heroes. Infpired by every generous Sentiment, thefe gallant Spirits founded Conftitutions, fhunned the Torrent of Corruption, battled for the State, ventured their Lives in the Defence of their Country, and glorioufly bled in the Caufe of Liberty.

Unfpotted Names, and memorable long,
If there be Force in Virtue, or in Song.

The Bufto's are placed in the following Order: The firft, and in the gable End of the Building, is Mr. *POPE.* The Gentleman (if a Gentleman, who left the following Lines on his Buft), beft knows what he meant by them :

For Love, fome worfhip ; fome for Fear :
Afk'ft Thou, my Friend, how *Pope* came here ?

The

The next, Sir *THOMAS GRESHAM*, with this Infcription :

Who, by the honourable Profeffion of a Merchant, having enriched himfelf, and his Country, for carrying on the Commerce of the World, built the *Royal Exchange*.

IGNATIUS JONES,

Who, to adorn his Country, introduced and rival'd the *Greek* and *Roman* Architecture.

JOHN MILTON,

Whofe fublime and unbounded Genius equalled a Subject that carried him beyond the Limits of the World.

WILLIAM SHAKESPEAR,

Whofe excellent Genius opened to him the whole Heart of Man, all the Mines of Fancy, all the Stores of Nature; and gave him Power, beyond all other Writers, to move, aftonifh, and delight Mankind.

JOHN

JOHN LOCKE,

Who, beft of all Philofophers, underftood the Powers of the human Mind, the Nature, End, and Bounds of Civil Government; and, with equal Courage and Sagacity, refuted the flavifh Syftems of ufurped Authority over the Rights, the Confciences, or the Reafon of Mankind.

Sir ISAAC NEWTON,

Whom the God of Nature made to comprehend his Works; and, from fimple Principles, to difcover the Laws never known before, and to explain the Appearances, never underftood, of this ftupendous Univerfe.

Sir FRANCIS BACON, Lord VERULAM,

Who, by the Strength and Light of a fuperior Genius, rejecting vain Speculation, and fallacious Theory, taught to purfue Truth, and improve Philofophy, by the certain Method of Experiment.

E 3

In

In the Niche of a Pyramid is placed a *Mercury*, with these Words subscrib'd :

—— *Campos ducit ad* Elysios.

—— Leads to th' *Elysian Fields.*

And below this Figure is fixed a Square of black Marble, with the following Lines :

Hic manus ob patriam pugnando vulnera passi,
Quique pii vates, & Phœbo digna locuti,
Inventas aut qui vitam excoluere per artes,
Quique sui memores alios fecere merendo.

Here are the Bands, who for their Country
          bled,
And Bards, whose pure and sacred Verse is
          read :
Those who, by Arts invented, Life improv'd,
And, by their Merits, made their Mem'ries
          lov'd.

KING *ALFRED,*

The mildest, justest, most beneficent of Kings ; who drove out the *Danes,* secured the Seas, protected Learning, established Juries,
                                        crushed

crufhed Corruption, guarded Liberty, and was the Founder of the *Englifh* Conftitution.

E D W A R D, Prince of *Wales*,

The Terror of *Europe*, the Delight of *England* ; who preferved, unaltered, in the Height of Glory and Fortune, his natural Gentlenefs and Modefty.

Queen *E L I Z A B E T H*,

Who confounded the Projects, and deftroyed the Power, that threatened to opprefs the Liberties of *Europe* ; took off the Yoke of Ecclefiaftical Tyranny ; reftored Religion from the Corruptions of Popery ; and, by a wife, a moderate, and a popular Government, gave Wealth, Security, and Refpect to *England*.

King *W I L L I A M* III.

Who, by his Virtue and Conftancy, having faved his Country from a Foreign Mafter, by a bold and generous Enterprize, preferved the Liberty and Religion of *Great Britain*.

Sir *WALTER RALEIGH*,

A valiant Soldier, and an able Statesman ; who, endeavouring to rouse the Spirit of his Master, for the Honour of his Country, against the Ambition of *Spain*, fell a Sacrifice to the Influence of that Court, whose Arms he had vanquished, and whose Designs he had opposed.

Sir *FRANCIS DRAKE*,

Who, through many Perils, was the First of *Britons* that adventured to sail round the Globe ; and carried into unknown Seas and Nations the Knowledge and Glory of the *English* Name.

JOHN HAMPDEN,

Who, with great Spirit, and consummate Abilities, began a noble Opposition to an arbitrary Court, in Defence of the Liberties of his Country ; supported them in Parliament ; and died for them in the Field.

Sir

Sir *JOHN BARNARD*,

Without any Infcription.

On the Backfide of this Building, is the
following Infcription :

To the Memory
of
SIGNIOR *FIDO*,
an *Italian* of good Extraction ;
who came into *England*,
not to bite us, like moft of his Countrymen,
but to gain an honeft Livelihood.
He hunted not after Fame,
yet acquir'd it :
regardlefs of the Praife of his Friends,
but moft fenfible of their Love.
Though he lived amongft the Great,
he neither learnt, nor flattered any Vice.
He was no Bigot :
Tho' he doubted of none of the 39 Articles.
And, if to follow Nature,
and to refpect the Laws of Society,
be Philofophy,
he was a perfect Philofopher ;
a faithful Friend,
an agreeable Companion,
a loving Hufband,
diftinguifhed by a numerous Offspring ;

all

all which he liv'd to fee take good Courfes.
In his old Age he retir'd
to the Houfe of a Clergyman in the Country ;
where he finifh'd his earthly Race,
and died an Honour and an Example to the
whole Species.
Reader,
this Stone is guiltlefs of Flattery :
For he to whom it is infcrib'd ·
was not a Man,
but a
GREY-HOUND.

Leaving this incomparable fweet Place with
great Regret, as every one who fees it muft,
we come to a *Gothic* Building, call'd

The TEMPLE of LIBERTY.

Libertati Majorum.
To the Liberty of our Anceftors.

It is an Imitation of a large antique Building of Brick, finely mimic, Seventy Feet
high, on the Summit of an Hill. It is impoffible to make a better Imitation of the antient Tafte of Architecture. This is a Kind of
Caftle, feveral Stories high, which commands
the whole Garden : One can never be tired
with beholding fo vaft and fo pleafing a Variety of Objects. The Windows are adorned
with curious Paintings upon Glafs in the
antique

Gothic Temple.

Buckinghamshire. abt 1750.

Page 40.

antique Tafte, and beautifully performed : On
the Infide of the Dome are the Arms of this
Family, from the Beginning to this prefent
Time ; and round it, on the Outfide, are
the Seven Statues mentioned before to have
been formerly placed round the *Saxon* Altar.
Here we have a boundlefs Profpect round the
Building, out of the Turrets, and on the
Ground likewife. From hence we defcend a
fine Hill, and on our Left-hand fee a Plan-
tation of Ever-greens ; on our Right, the
well-defigned Walks and Groves, not finifhed
nor grown. From thence you perceive to
the Right a large Piece of Ground, which my
Lord defigns for new Improvements ; and, on
which, he has feveral Men at Work : But, as
I do not know his Plan, I can fay nothing to
you upon that Subject. Certain, however, it
is, that to form a Judgment by the Proofs
he has already given of his Tafte and Magnificence, thofe new Embellifhments cannot but
be of the fame Stamp. But, to return to our
Gothic Caftle ; within, you fee not the leaft
Ornament ; and yet there is an extraordinary
Pleafure in this antique Simplicity. The
whole Edifice feems old, and is left unfinifh-
ed : In this a great deal of Art is difcovered.
Round it are placed on Pedeftals a vaft Number of Bufts, reprefenting the old *Saxon* Deities ; and thefe Bufts feem quite antique, tho'
they are intirely modern. At a little Diftance
you fee carrying on a grand Building in the
Greek

Greek Tafte, which is to be called *Une Maifon du* ———, and the Walks on each Side are not laid out ; but their Intention, I believe, is to lengthen out by the Side of a clofe Vifta an open grand Terras. It is a Kind of Pain to quit fuch amufing and agreeable Objects ! But you are foon made eafy, upon entering a charming Temple, call'd,

The LADIES TEMPLE.

This is a handfome Structure of Free-ftone, the Floor of which is only a Portico open on all Sides upon Arches, with *Venetian* Windows : A very neat Stair-cafe leads to a Hall, where every thing ravifhes the Eye, particularly the extreme Elegancy and Beauty of the Ornaments. On the Right-hand are Ladies employing themfelves in Needle and Shell-work. On the oppofite Side, are Ladies diverting themfelves with Painting and Mufic. They are painted in Oil by Mr. *Slater* : And the other Embellifh-ments reprefent all manner of Exercifes fuit-able to the Fair Sex. Here the Painter feems to have defignedly drawn none but tempting Features, and amiable Countenances. Not far from hence is a Monument erected to the Memory of Captain *Grenville*, with this In-fcription :

Sororis

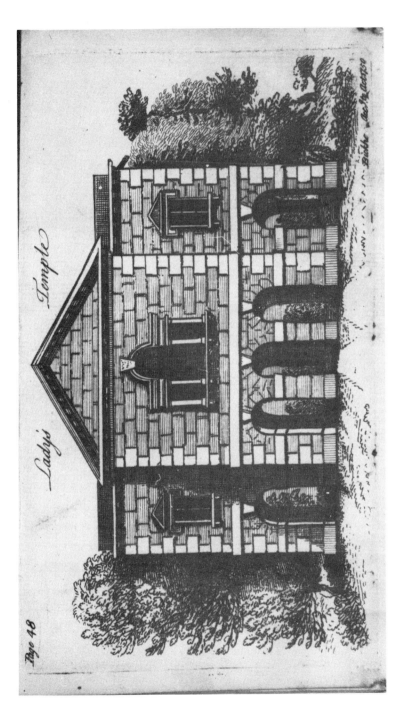

Page 48

Lady's Temple

Grecian Temple

Bickham

Capt: Grenville's Monument

Acc. to Act.

Sororis suæ Filio
Thomæ Grenville
Qui navis præfectus regiæ,
Ducente classem Britannicam Georgio Anson,
Dum contra Gallos *fortissimè pugnaret,*
Dilaceratæ navis ingenti fragmine
Femore graviter percusso,
Perire, dixit moribundus, omnino satius esse,
Quam inertiæ reum in judicio sisti ;
Columnam hanc rostratam
Laudans & mærens posuit
Cobham.
Insigne virtutis, eheu ! rarissimæ
Exemplum habes ;
Ex quo discas
Quid virum præfectura militari ornatum
Deceat.
M.DCC.XLVII.

To his Sister's Son,
Thomas Grenville,
Who, being Captain of a Ship in the Royal
Navy,
(when *George Anson* commanded the *British*
Fleet)
whilst he fought gallantly against the *French*,
and had a severe Stroke on his Thigh,
with a large Splinter of the shatter'd Vessel,
declar'd it in his last Moments, infinitely better
to perish,
than be brought to Judgment for Cowardice :
F   Is

Is this Pillar, representing his Manner of Life,
as an Approbation of his Conduct,
as well as Concern for his own Loss,
erected by
Cobham.
Here, alas ! you have a remarkable Example
of the most distinguish'd Bravery ;
from which may be learnt,
what Qualifications are requisite for a Man
honour'd with a Military Command.
1747.

Not far from this, and up a grand Walk, I
am leading you now to that genteel Piece of
Building, which goes by the Name of

The *PALLADIAN* BRIDGE.

This is a very handsome Bridge over one of
the Rivers : The Roof on the Side facing the
Water is supported by *Ionic* Columns ; the
Backside of it by an *Alto-Relievo* of the Four
Quarters of the World (finely carved by *Rys-
brach*), bringing their Products to *Britannia.*
Here are, besides, a great many modern and
antique Bustoes of Marble : On each Side of
the *Alto-Relievo* are painted by Mr. *Sleter*, in
Fresco, Sir *Walter Raleigh* with a Map of *Virginia* in his Hand, and Sir *William Penn* hold-
ing the Laws of *Pensylvania.* This Bridge
has a most delightful Effect, when beheld
from

from so many different Parts of this magnificent Garden : It is a covered and vaulted Fabric, where you see the different Parts of the World bringing their several Products to *Britain* (as taken notice of before), to whom they seem to pay Homage. A great many of these Figures are extremely striking. There is so much Art required, and so much Difficulty attends doing any-thing in this Way, as it ought to be, that when we do meet with a good Piece of Workmanship of this Kind, it affords us an extreme Pleasure : But I must confess, I should rather have found Sir *William* among the *British* Worthies. This same *Penn*, I assure you, is a great Favourite ; I esteem him one of the most worthy Legislators upon Record : His Laws, I am told, act still with great Force in *Pensylvania*, and keep the honest inoffensive People there in extreme good Order. Our Sailors mention his Colony as a very happy Set of People ; they live intirely at Peace amongst themselves ; and (bred up in a strict Observance of Probity), without the least Knowledge of any Art Military amongst them, are able to preserve the most sociable Terms with their Neighbours. There are Bustoes, as was said before, some are Originals, and the others very good ; but there is such an absurd Taste in the Sculptor's ridiculous Humour to make these party-coloured Faces, by the Veins of different Colours that run through the Marble, that I cannot con-

ceive

ceive how it fhould ever enter into his Head fo
ridiculoufly to make every Feature of a Man's
Face of a different Colour ; and it amazes me,
that we daily fee fo many Inftances of the
like Abfurdities.   Near this Bridge is

The IMPERIAL CLOSET:

Which is a fquare Room, in which are painted by Mr. *Sleter* a noble Triumvirate of the
worthieft of the *Roman* Emperors ; who are
diftinguifhed each by a memorable Saying of
his own fixed over him. *Titus, Trajan,* and
Aurelius, are Names which want not Pomp of
Title to add a Luftre to them. Over the
Head of one of them is written that beautiful
Maxim, relating to the Sword worn by Sove-
reigns, *Let it be for me, if I deferve it ; but
againft me, if I am unworthy.*

Imp. Titus Cæf. Vefpafian.

Diem perdidi.————I have loft a Day.

Imp. N. Trajan. Cæf. Aug.

Pro me : fi merear, in me.

For me : But, if I deferve it, againft me.

Imp.

Imperial Closet.

Rotherham Sc. oct. 1773.

Page 53

Temple of Friendship

Bickham dec. 9 D Oct 177..

Imp. Marcus Aurelius Cæfar Antoninus.
Ita regnes Imperator, ut privatus regi te velis.

So govern, when an Emperor, as, if a private
Perfon, you would defire to be governed.

From hence you pafs into the great Terras-
Walk, which is 3000 Feet long: You go by
a noble Iron Gate at the End, which leads
you to

The TEMPLE of FRIENDSHIP.

With this Motto on the Outfide :

Amicitiæ S.————————Sacred to Frindfhip.

It is a lofty fquare Building, of the *Doric*
Order; with Three noble Porticoes on the
Sides, which appear to the Garden. This is
a Structure of a noble Tafte, and very elegantly adorned. It is full of illuftrious
Bufts, but not one Monarch amongft them;
perhaps to hint, that this Set of Men does
not feem to be formed to love, and much
lefs to be loved : Be that as it will, I
was highly pleafed to find fuch Company.
For around the Room are placed Ten Pedeftals, for the Bufts of his Lordfhip, and
Nine of his felect Friends ; *viz.* the Prince

F 3   of

of *Wales.*—Earls of *Westmorland, Chesterfield,*
and *Marchmont.*—Lords *Cobham, Gower,* and
Bathurst.—*Richard Grenville, William Pitt,* and
George Lyttelton, Esqrs.—— This is elegant, I
must confess ; these Busts are all well done,
and some of them very well, by *Ryſbrack ;*
and I am extremely taken likewise with the
Painting, which is by Mr. *Sleter :* That Em-
blem of Friendſhip above the Door, thoſe
of Juſtice, and Liberty ; and thoſe other Ornaments upon the Walls, are well touched ;
and that Emblematic Painting on the Cieling.
There, you ſee, ſits *Britannia :* Upon one Side
is held the Glory of her Annals on Cartoons,
whereon theſe Words are written, *The Reigns
of Queen* Elizabeth *and* Edward III. and on
the other is offered the Reign of ———,
which ſhe frowns upon, and puts by. The
Name is artfully covered with *Britannia's*
Hand ; but it is an eaſy Matter to gueſs what
Reign is meant. Excellent ! upon my Word :
Faith, it is good ! Never accept it, honeſt
Lady, till Corruption is at an End, and public Spirit revive. Then going out of this
Temple, and as we walk along the Terras,
you may obſerve the great Advantage of low
Walls : By this means the Garden is extended
beyond its Limits, and takes in every thing
entertaining, that is to be met with in the
Range of half a Country. Villages, Works
of Huſbandry, Groups of Cattle, Herds of
Deer, and a Variety of other beautiful Objects,

jects, are brought into the Garden, and make a Part of the Place. Even to the *nicest* Taste these rural Scenes are highly delightful; for whoever has no Relish for them, gives Reason for a Suspicion, that he has no Taste at all.

Strait mine Eye hath caught new Pleasures,
Whilst the Landschape round it measures,
Russet Lawns, and Fallows grey,
Where the nibbling Flocks do stray:
Mountains, on whose barren Breast
The lab'ring Clouds do often rest:
Meadows trim, with Daisies py'd,
Shallow Brooks, and Rivers wide:
Tow'rs and Battlements it sees,
Bosom'd high in tufted Trees:
Where, perhaps, some Beauty lies,
The Cynosure of neighb'ring Eyes.
Hard by a Cottage-Chimney smokes,
From betwixt Two aged Oaks.

It must be owned indeed, that these Walks want such Opening into the Country as little as any Place can well be imagined to do: Yet even *Stow* itself, I assure you, is much improved by them. They contrast beautifully with this more polished Nature, and set it off to greater Advantage. The Eye, after surfeiting itself with the Feast here provided for it, by using a little Exercise in travelling about the Country, grows hungry again, and returns to the Entertainment with fresh Appetite.

tite. Besides, there is nothing so distasteful
to the Eye as a confined Prospect (where the
Reasonableness of it does not appear); especially if a dead Wall, or any other such disagreeable Object, steps in between. The Eye
naturally loves Liberty, and when it is in quest
of Prospects, will not rest content with the
most beautiful Dispositions of Art, confined
within a narrow Compass; but (as soon as
the Novelty of Sights is over) will begin again
to grow dissatisfied, till the whole Limits of
the Horizon be given it to range through.
The Eye is like a Bee. Plant as many Flowers
as you will near its Hive, yet still the little
Insect will be discontented, unless it be allowed to wander o'er the Country, and be
its own Caterer. But we will continue our
Walk: I look upon that Statue, call'd *the
Gladiator*, as one of the finest in the World:
I wish I had seen the Original; for the Posture
to me here always appears a little too much
strained. I can scarce throw myself into such
an Attitude. Yet it is fine, I must confess.
You have the best View of it from hence:
Most of the Engravings, I have met with,
give us the back View; but, I think, the Statue
appears infinitely to the best Advantage,
when taken in Front: The Air of the Head
is delightful, and cannot be hid, without de-
priving the Figure of half its Life. But, to
return to our Walk, just here in a neat Recess, is

The

Pebble Work &c.

Brookham Watering & Co 1730

The PEBBLE ALCOVE.

It is a little Grot, neatly adorned with Pebbles: His Lordſhip's Arms are curiouſly wrought upon the Back-wall with the ſame Materials, and diſplayed in proper Colours, which has a very pretty and agreeable Effect; but you will not here, nor any-where about the Garden (except the Obeliſk, deſign'd for a *Jet d'Eau*, taken notice of before), find any ſuch thing as Water-ſpouts, nor Orangeries, nor Parterres, nor other ſymmetrical Toys. For, on the one hand, the *Engliſh* cannot bear that tireſome Regularity of Parterries, nor that prodigious Number of Flowers, which often affect the Head, and incommode more than they pleaſe: To all this Form they prefer fine Graſs-plats, and ſpacious Lawns, with beautiful Alleys of Trees, large Pieces of Water, and wide Viſta's, diverſified a thouſand Ways. On the other Side, as my Lord's Plan is not yet completed, perhaps he ſtill intends to have ſome Waterworks; which are, doubtleſs, ſome of the fineſt Ornaments of a Garden; and, to his, would add the laſt Degree of Perfection. It is not Water that is wanting; for there is Plenty of it: And I queſtion whether the Expence would retard the Work, ſince there is ſo great a Profuſion in every thing elſe; a Profuſion, that ſavours more of a Sovereign, than of a
Britiſh

Britiſh Peer. Now, as you walk along, you come to

CONGREVE's MONUMENT.

The Embelliſhments round it are deſigned to expreſs the Poet's Genius in the Dramatic Way ; and, at the Top of it, is placed a Monkey beholding himſelf in a Mirror ; and, under him, this Writing :

> *Vitæ imitatio,*
> *Conſuetudinis ſpeculum,*
> *Comœdia.*

Comedy is the Imitation of Life, and the Mirror of Faſhion.

The Poet's Effigies lies in a careleſs Poſture on one Side ; and on the other is placed this Epitaph :

> *Ingenio*
> *Acri, faceto, expolito,*
> *Moribuſque*
> *Urb anis, candidis, facillimis,*
> *Gulielmi Congreve,*
> *Hoc*
> *Qualecunque deſiderii ſui*
> *Solamen ſimul &*
>   *Monumentum*

Congreve's Monument

Bickham *According to Act* 1760.

Page 59.

To preserve the Memory   of her Husband
        Ann Viscountess   Cobham,
Caused this Pillar to be   erected in the Year 1747

Birkham Arch to Act 1750

Monumentum
Posuit Cobham.
1736.

To the piercing, elegant, polished
Wit,
and civilized, candid, most unaffected
Manners,
of *William Congreve*,
hath *Cobham* erected
this poor Consolation for, as well as
Monument of, his Loss.
1736.

Now, as these Parts of the Gardens are un-
finished, if we have the Pleasure of your
Company in this Country next Year, you will
see, I dare say, great Alterations here; for
that Base yonder is to shoot up into a lofty
Monument, in the Taste of that at *London*,
but not quite so big; intended for a Statue
of my Lord on the Top of it, and dedicated
by my Lady to his Memory: And several of
those Objects you see before you, are to take
new Forms upon them. A little higher, we
have a good View into the Country from
hence. Those Woods are extremely elegant
in their Kind; we must be contented with
only beholding them at present: They seem,
at this Distance, to be laid out in a very fine
Manner, and cut into very beautiful Ridings,
which

which are Eight or Ten Miles round : These
are the noble Production of Art and Nature.
I think every End is answered, when a Nation's
Taste is regulated, with regard to the most
innocent, the most refined, and elegant of its
Pleasures.   In all polite Countries, the Amuse-
ments of the People were thought highly de-
serving a Legislature's Inspection. To establish
a just Taste in these, was esteemed in some
measure, as advancing the Success of Virtue :
And can it be considered, as a Work intirely of a private Nature, for a superior Genius
to exert itself in an Endeavour to fix a true
Standard of Beauty in any of these allowed
and useful Kinds of Pleasures ? In that of
Gardening particularly, the Taste of the Nation has long been so depraved, that I think
we might be obliged to any one that would
undertake to reform it : While a Taste for
Painting, Music, Architecture, and other polite Arts, in some measure, prevailed among
us, our Gardens, for the most part, were laid
out in so formal, aukward, and wretched a
Manner, that they were really a Scandal to the
Genius of the Nation : A Man of Taste was
shocked whenever he set his Foot into them.
But *Stow*, it is to be hoped, may work some
Reformation: I would have our Country
'Squires flock hither two or three times a
Year, by way of Improvement ; and, after
they have looked about them a little, return
home with new Notions, and begin to see
the

Keeper's Lodge in the Park.

Castle

Bickham according to Act 1750.

the Abfurdity of their clipped Yews, their Box-wood Borders, their flourifhed Parterres, and their lofty Brick-walls. For to me, I muft own, there appears a very vifible Connexion between an improved Tafte for Pleafure, and a Tafte for Virtue. When I fit ravifhed at an Oratorio, or ftand aftonifhed before the Cartoons, or enjoy myfelf in thefe happy Walks, I can feel my Mind expand itfelf, my Notions inlarge, and my Heart better difpofed either for a religious Thought, or a benevolent Action. In a word, I cannot help imagining a Tafte for thefe exalted Pleafures contributes towards making me a better Man : Befides, there is another Advantage in Wealth laid out in this elegant Manner, which is this: The Money fpent in the Neighbourhood, by the Company daily crouding hither, to fatisfy their Curiofity. There is a kind of continual Fair ; and I have heard feveral of the Inhabitants fay, that it is one of the beft Trades they have: Their Inns, their Shops, their Farms, and Shambles, all find their Account in it: So that, in my Opinion, viewed in this Light only, fuch Productions of Art may be confidered as a very great Advantage to every Neighbourhood, that enjoys the lucky Situation of being placed near them. To this Advantage might be added, the great Degree of Pleafure from hence derived

rived

rived daily to such Numbers of People. A Place like this, is a kind of keeping open House: There is a Repast at all Times ready for the Entertainment of Strangers. And sure, if there is any Degree of Benevolence, you must think an useful End answered in thus affording an innocent Gratification to so many Fellow-Creatures. A *Sunday* Evening spent here, adds a new Relish to the Day of Rest, and makes the Sabbath appear more chearful to the Labourer, after a toilsome Week. For my Part, I assure you, I have scarce experienced a greater Pleasure, than I have often felt, upon meeting a Variety of pleased Faces in these Walks. All Care and Uneasiness seem to be left behind at the Garden-Door, and People enter here fully resolved to enjoy themselves, and the several beautiful Objects around them. In one Part, a Face presents itself marked with the Passion of gaping Wonder; in another, you meet a Countenance bearing the Appearance of a more rational Pleasure; and in a third, a Set of Features composed into serene Joy; whilst the Man of Taste is seen examining every Beauty with a curious Eye, and discovering his Approbation in a half-formed Smile. To this I might still add another Advantage of a public Nature, derived from these elegant Productions of Art; and that is, their Tendency to raise us in the Opinion of Fo-

reigners. If our Nation had nothing of this Kind to boast of, all our Neighbours would look upon us as a stupid tasteless Set of People, and not worth visiting: So that, for the Credit of the Country, I think, something of this Kind ought to be exhibited amongst us. Our public Virtues, if we have any, would not, I dare say, appear to less Advantage, when recommended by these Embellishments of Art. I decline mentioning several other Ornaments, with which this spacious Garden is embellished; likewise several remarkable Statues. It is impossible for a Traveller, who has only two or three Days to make so many Drawings of each particular Building, and to run through so great Variety of Beauties, not to let something escape his Curiosity, or to remember exactly all he has seen; but by the Help of Drawing you may carry a great deal more away with you, than by Memory: Which is the Reason why I thought this Work would be acceptable to the Public; which will undoubtedly refresh their Memory in each Particular, and likewise give a more strong Idea of the Whole: And, in order to refresh my own Memory, I have made use of some Descriptions already printed, which are distributed to those who will have them, at *Stow.* I have now gone round, and given you a faint Description, and Sketches in Light and Shadow, of this
un-

unparallel'd Chain of artificial and natural Beauty ; and, to make ufe of Two Lines, which will not be thought improper :

Here Order in Variety you fee,
Where all Things differ, yet where all agree.

Such are the inchanting Gardens of *Stow* : But I have made no mention as yet of the Houfe. This is a handfome modern Structure, the Infide not yet finifhed. The Architecture is *Italian*, and in a very elegant Tafte. The Houfe is large, and decorated with a Row of Pillars in the Middle of the firft Story, which you come up to by a noble Flight of Stone Steps : On each Side it is fupported with Two Pavilions fomewhat lower, though on the fame Front ; and thefe by Two fmaller Pavilions, placed in the fame manner, and adorned with Columns ; which, in the whole Length, is Ninety odd Yards long ; and forms a fuperb Front, which takes in the whole Opening of the great Alley, and rather more by the inner Row of Arbail-Trees ; which, if cut down, the Houfe would appear to greater Advantage. When you are in this Houfe, or rather Palace, afcending by a magnificent Stair-cafe (which is finely painted by Mr. *Sleter*), you enter fome of the fineft Rooms perhaps in *Europe*. I will not take up your
Time

Time with a Defcription of the Apartments and Furniture of this coftly Fabric: I fhall be contented with informing you, that every thing is in the modern and moft fuperb Tafte. Gilded Carvings, Glaffes and Sconces, without Number; fine wrought Frames, well-painted Cielings, Variety of Pictures, on all Subjects, by the ableft Mafters; Marble Bufts, Statues, curious Chimneys, elegant Tables, rich Hangings and Tapeftry, gilded Furniture. There are fome fine Bas-relievos; but, in particular, there is one Piece of Alt-relief ftruck me beyond every thing: The Story is *Darius's* Tent; and it is fo charmingly told, that I have had, I can affure you, a meaner Opinion of *Le Brun* upon that Subject, ever fince I have feen it: The Compofition is fo juft, the Figures fo graceful and correct, the Paffions fo ftriking, nay, the very Drapery fo free and eafy, that I declare I was altogether aftonifhed at the Sight of it.

In fhort, whatever can be imagined in the moft agreeable and richeft Tafte, is lavifhed, as it were, in this noble Building.

At length, I have done with *Stow*, the Wonder of our Days, and the moft charming Place in all *England!* There is fcarce a Traveller, of ever fo little Tafte or Curiofity, that, upon coming to *London*, does not pay a Vifit to *Blenheim*; but efpecially to *Stow*, as the moft fplendid and magnificent Ornament of
this

this fine wealthy Country. I was struck with
the Majesty of *Blenheim* House; and though,
I must own, it appeared to me more sump-
tuous than graceful, yet I could not help admiring the Beauty of the Apartments, the
Richness of the Ornaments and Paintings;
but especially the fine Gallery, containing the
Duke of *Marlborough's* Library: Besides, I
was charmed with the lovely Prospect, formed by the Bridge, the River, the Column
erected in Honour of the great Duke of
Marlborough, and by all the neighbouring
Landschape. But all falls short of *Stow.* I
own, indeed, that the famous Garden of Sir
Jeremy Sambrook, at *Gubbins* in the County of
Hertford, deserves a Traveller's Admiration;
and that you there see a sensible Resemblance
in Miniature of *Stow.* For Example: Imagine
to yourself a vast Hill, shaded all over with a
Forest of Oaks, through which have been
cut an infinite Number of Alleys covered
with the finest Gravel. Here you meet with
a Grotto agreeably adorned, in which is
heard the gentle Murmur of a Cascade, surrounded with tufted Trees. There you come
to a large Square, embellished with Orange-
trees and Statues, and with a beautiful Sum-
mer-house, whose Windows present on
every Side a most delicious Prospect. Now
you behold a magnificent Bason, adorned with
green Pyramids, Orange-trees, Statues, and
surrounded

furrounded with wide-extending Alleys ; and then you fee a kind of verdant Circle, all covered with the Trees of the Foreft, but illumined with fo much Art and Tafte, as to fill the Eye with Raptures. In fhort, the Beauty of the Alleys, whofe verdant Hedges are of a furprifing Height, the pleafing Variety of the Profpects, the Richnefs of the Orna-ments, the fingular Tafte that prevails through the whole Diftribution, and the Choice of the different Parts of this charming Place, form all together almoft the only Garden in its Kind. But, notwithftanding all the furprifing Greatnefs of *Gubbins*, ftill it muft fubmit to *Stow*.

F I N I S.

PRINTS,

AND

BOOKS,

Sold in *May*'s Buildings, *Covent-Garden.*

Printed for GEORGE BICKHAM, Engraver, late Drawing-Master to the Academy at *Greenwich.*

(Where all Sorts of Picture-Work, as well as Writing and Shopkeepers Bills, are executed in a neat Manner, and at the most reasonable Rates. Authors and Booksellers may have Frontispieces, and Cuts for Books, designed, drawn, and engraved in the best Taste, and printed in the cleanest Manner, to produce a beautiful Impression, at the lowest Prices: As also Pictures neatly framed and glazed. Likewise all Gentlemen, Merchants, City, and Country Shopkeepers may be furnished at the best Hand.)

BOOKS.

1. Deliciæ Britannicæ : Or the Curiosities of *Hampton-Court,* and *Windsor-Castle* ; delineated with occasional Reflections, and embellished with Copper-Plates of the two Palaces, &c. (a necessary Pocket-Companion for such as visit those Courts ; the Whole attempted with a View, not only to engage the Attention of the Curious, but to inform the Judgments of those who have the least Taste for the Art of Painting. Second Edition. Bound 2s. 6d. To be continued through the Courts.

2. The Usefulness of the Stage to Religion and Government: Also a Distinction between the Stage and the Press ; with a Front-spiece. 1s.

3. The Life and Death of Pierce Gaveston, Earl of Cornwall, Grand Favourite, and Prime Minister : With political Remarks by

way

way of Caution to all Crown'd Heads, and evil Ministers : With a curious Frontispiece in a political Taste. 1 s.

4. An Introduction to Dancing : Or genteel Behaviour fully explained by Twelve Figures in Dancing Positions, drawn from the Life, and printed Directions ; with Twelve new Minuets and Rigadoons, never before publish'd. The Musick by an eminent Hand. 1 s.

5. A short Trip into Kent : Containing the Occurrences of four Summer Days ; calculated as an Antidote against the Gloominess of the Winter Months ; and particularly that which is occasioned by the Observation of the 30th of January, in Hudibrastick Verse. Price 6 d.

6. The Art of Fortification delineated ; with Rules for Designing, Drawing, Washing and Colouring in the most elegant Taste, particular Works and Buildings, and their Plans, Elevations, Sections, Profiles and Fronts, in civil and military Architecture : As likewise the intire Survey of a Place, with its particular Charts, and the Description of Provinces, States, Kingdoms, Empires, &c. A Work absolutely necessary for the Gentleman, Officer, and Architect. Adorn'd with Twenty-three Cuts, engrav'd by G. Bickham.

BOOKS Engraved.

7. Oeconomy of Arts, a new Drawing, Japanning, and Writing-Book ; being a curious Display of those Arts, in a more accurate Manner than any thing of the like Kind hitherto extant ; by which the young Practitioner is gradually led from the first Elements of each, to the Performance, in a short time, of the most finished Pieces. 2 s. separate. 6 s. the whole.

8. The New-Year's Gift : Or, Time's Progress for the Year 1748, 1749, 1750, adorn'd with Figures and Habits to each Month, with the Signs of the Zodiack, and useful Observations on the Day of the Week, Husbandry, and the Season ; with a Description under each Month. 1 s.

9. The whole Opera of Flora, with the humorous Scenes of Hob ; 28 Pages being so many Songs. The Pictures design'd by Mr. Gravelot, and engraved with the Musick ; and a new Bass and Thorough-Bass, by Mr. Howard, proper for all Instruments. 2 s.

10. The Opera of the Devil to pay ; with the Scenes engraved in Picture-Work on the Top of each Song, and the Speech that introduces them : The Musick, and a new Bass, by Mr. Vincent, proper for all Instruments. 6 d.

11. Six Folio Songs new, decorated with Pictures. 6 d.

12. The first Principles of Geometry explained ; with a whimsical Picture to each Page. 1 s. bound and gilt.

13. A new Book of twelve of the most famous Running-Horses, drawn from the Life by Wotton, Tellemens, &c. in Quarto ; viz. The Bloody-shoulder'd Arabian, belonging to the Right Hon. the Earl of Oxford ; Childers, belonging to the Duke of Devonshire : Camillus, a Horse belonging to the Duke of Bolton ; Windham, a Horse belonging to the Duke of Somerset ; Victorious, a Horse belonging

longing to the Earl of Portmore: Lempere, a Horse belonging to the late Sir William Morgan: Silver-Locks, a Mare belonging to the Earl of Godolphin: Sir Rob. F——g tempting a Country-Girl with his Purse: Fearnought, a Horse belonging to the Duke of Bolton. A View of a Horse-Match at Newmarket, and of a Rubbing-House. Chanters upon full Stretch. The standing Leap at the Bar. These all of a Size. Price 1 s. 6 d.

15 An Account Book, by way of Debtor and Creditor; with an alphabetical Index to turn at one to any Person's Name Pr

16 The Gentleman's Memorandum-Book, engraved Price 2 s

17 The Ladies Memorandum-Book, containing 104 Pages, for every Day, Week, and Month throughout the Year, for the Use and Convenience of all People; particularly to set down their Expences, Engagements, Memorandums, Messages, or occasional Business, and other Occurrences Price 2 s 6 d or 1 s 6 d

18 A monthly Calendar; a Column of each Day of the Month, of a very neat little Size, to set down any particular thing therein, Curiously engraved on Copper-Plates. Price 2 s 6 d bound

19 Tom Thumb turn'd Wizard; or the little Masters and Misses large Folio Conjuring Book; containing all the Birds in the Air, and all the Beasts on the Earth, with Explanations Price 2 s

20 Silent Converse; or the little Master's and Misses Finger-Book; shewing how to discourse together by their Fingers only, and as well in the Dark as the Light Price bound 6 d

21 The Beau Mode; or the Bath, Tunbridge, and Scarborough Portraits, being Twenty Animal Heads and their Likeness; with the Round Heads; Flat Heads; Short Heads; Long Heads; Straight Heads; Corve Heads; Broad Heads; and Narrow Heads, engraved on Copper-Plates Price 2 s

22 Four Dice, containing Twenty-four Letters; being an Alphabet to teach Children their A, B, C. The Four Dice above-mentioned, I think so easy and useful, that it will be hard to find any better Way to make this kind of Learning a Sport to cozen them into the Knowledge of the Letters they will be taught to read, without perceiving it to be any thing but a Play-thing Price 6 d

23 The Dominical Rutula; (inscribed to the Hon. Leslie, Esq; Brother to the Right Hon. John Earl of Rothes; by his Honour's most humble, Servant, James Leslie) being a perpetual Kalendar, to know any particular Day of the Month or Week, either backwards or forwards for many hundred Years, with a Description. Price 1 s

WILLIAM ANDREWS CLARK
MEMORIAL LIBRARY

UNIVERSITY OF CALIFORNIA, LOS ANGELES

The Augustan Reprint Society

PUBLICATIONS IN PRINT

The Augustan Reprint Society

PUBLICATIONS IN PRINT

141. Sir Roger L'Estrange, Selections from *The Observator* (1681-1687).
142. Anthony Collins, *A Discourse Concerning Ridicule and Irony In Writing* (1729).
143. *A Letter From a Clergyman to His Friend, with an Account of the Travels of Captain Lemuel Gulliver* (1726).
144. *The Art of Architecture, A Poem* (1742).

1970-1971
145-146. Thomas Shelton, *A Tutor to Tachygraphy, or Short-writing* (1642) and *Tachygraphy* (1647).
147-148. *Deformities of Dr. Samuel Johnson* (1782).
149. *Poeta de Tristibus: or the Poet's Complaint* (1682).
150. Gerard Langbaine, *Momus Triumphans: or the Plagiaries of the English Stage* (1687).

1971-1972
151-152. Evan Lloyd, *The Methodist. A Poem* (1766).
153. *Are These Things So?* (1740), and *The Great Man's Answer to Are These Things So?* (1740).
154. Arbuthnotiana: *The Story of the St. Alb-ns Ghost* (1712), and *A Catalogue of Dr. Arbuthnot's Library* (1779).
155-156. *A Selection of Emblems from Herman Hugo's Pia Desideria* (1624), with English Adaptations by Francis Quarles and Edmund Arwaker.

1972-1973
157. William Mountfort, *The Life and Death of Doctor Faustus* (1697).
158. Colley Cibber, *A Letter from Mr. Cibber to Mr. Pope* (1742).
159. [Catherine Clive] *The Case of Mrs. Clive* (1744).
160. [Thomas Tryon] *A Discourse ... of Phrensie, Madness or Distraction from A Treatise of Dreams and Visions* [1689].
161. Robert Blair, *The Grave. A Poem* (1743).
162. [Bernard Mandeville] *A Modest Defence of Publick Stews* (1724).

1973-1974
163. [William Rider] *An Historical and Critical Account of the Lives and Writings of the Living Authors of Great Britain* (1762).
164. Thomas Edwards, *The Sonnets of Thomas Edwards* (1765, 1780).
165. Hildebrand Jacob, *Of the Sister Arts: An Essay* (1734).
166. *Poems on the Reign of William III* [1690, 1696, 1699, 1702].
167. Kane O'Hara, *Midas: An English Burletta* (1766).
168. [Daniel Defoe] *A Short Narrative History of the Life and Actions of His Grace John, D. of Marlborough* (1711).

1974-1975

169-170. Samuel Richardson, *The Apprentice's Vade-Mecum* (1734).

171. James Bramston, *The Man of Taste* (1733).

172-173. Walter Charleton, *The Ephesian Matron* (1668).

174. Bernard Mandeville, *The Mischiefs That Ought Justly to be Appre* hended From a Whig-Government (1714).

174X. John Melton, *Astrologaster* (1620).

1975-1976

175. *Pamela Censured* (1741).

176. William Gilpin, *Dialogue upon the Gardens . . . at Stowe* (1748).

177. James Bramston, *Art of Politicks* (1729).

178. James Miller, *Harlequin-Horace or the Art of Modern Poetry* (1731).

179. [James Boswell] *View of the Edinburgh Theatre during the Summer Season, 1759* (1760).

180. Satires on Women: Robert Gould, *Love Given O're* (1682); Sarah Fige, *The Female Advocate* (1686); and Richard Ames, *The Folly of Love* (1691).

Publications of the first eighteen years of the society (numbers 1 - 108) are available in paperbound units of six issues at $16.00 per unit, from Kraus Reprint Company, Route 100, Millwood, New York 10546.

Publications in print are available at the regular membership rate of $5.00 for individuals and $8.00 for institutions per year. Prices of single issues may be obtained upon request. Subsequent publications may be checked in the annual prospectus.

Make check or money order payable to

THE REGENTS OF THE UNIVERSITY OF CALIFORNIA

and send to

The William Andrews Clark Memorial Library
2520 Cimarron Street, Los Angeles, California 90018